SECOND GEOLOGICAL SURVEY OF PENNSYLVANIA: 1874.

SPECIAL REPORT

ON THE

PETROLEUM OF PENNSYLVANIA,

ITS

PRODUCTION, TRANSPORTATION, MANUFACTURE AND STATISTICS.

BY HENRY E. WRIGLEY.

WITH

MAPS AND ILLUSTRATIONS.

TO WHICH ARE ADDED

A MAP AND PROFILE OF A LINE OF LEVELS THROUGH BUTLER, ARMSTRONG AND CLARION COUNTIES.

BY D. JONES LUCAS.

AND ALSO

A MAP AND PROFILE OF A LINE OF LEVELS ALONG SLIPPERY ROCK CREEK.

BY J. P. LESLEY.

HARRISBURG:
PUBLISHED BY THE BOARD OF COMMISSIONERS
FOR THE SECOND GEOLOGICAL SURVEY.
1875.

Electrotyped by
COLLINS & M'CLEESTER,
PHILADELPHIA.

Printed by
B. F. MEYERS, *State Printer*,
HARRISBURG, PA.

BOARD OF COMMISSIONERS.

His Excellency, JOHN F. HARTRANFT, *Governor*,
and *ex-officio* President of the Board, Harrisburg.

ARIO PARDEE, - - - - - - - Hazleton.
WILLIAM A. INGHAM, - - - - Philadelphia.
HENRY S. ECKERT, - - - - - Reading.
HENRY M'CORMICK, - - - - - Harrisburg.
JAMES MACFARLANE, - - - - - Towanda.
JOHN B. PEARSE, - - - - - Philadelphia.
ROBERT B. WILSON, M. D., - - - Clearfield.
Hon. DANIEL J. MORRELL, - - - Johnstown.
HENRY W. OLIVER, - - - - - Pittsburg.
SAMUEL Q. BROWN, - - - - - Pleasantville.

SECRETARY OF THE BOARD

JOHN B. PEARSE, - - - - - Philadelphia.

STATE GEOLOGIST

PETER LESLEY, - - - - - - Philadelphia.

TITUSVILLE, PA., *December* 31, 1874.

Professor J. P. LESLEY,

State Geologist:

DEAR SIR:—In obedience to the instructions received from you, I respectfully present the following report upon the Oil Regions of Pennsylvania.

Trusting that the nature of the work at this stage of the survey, will obtain consideration for whatever incompleteness it may possess.

I remain,

Very truly yours,

HENRY E. WRIGLEY, *C. E.*

CONTENTS.

DESCRIPTION OF THE MAPS.

Map A.—Showing the entire oil producing regions of the eastern United States, together with the relative position and areas of the four main oil regions, Canada, Pennsylvania, Ohio and Kentucky.

Showing also the water shed of the country, the summit line near the Lake, and the relative situation of Pennsylvania.

Map B.—The Pennsylvania oil regions proper, with all adjoining developments in Ohio, New York and West Virginia.

The present oil centres outlined and defined, under their separate and special names, and the outlying developments numbered and described.

A section giving an outline of the relative situation of the oil bearing sands from Lake Erie to the Ohio river. (Printed separately.)

Plate A.—Plan of a well rig and tools for artesian drilling, (with details,) as in use at present in the Pennsylvania region.

A map and profile of a line of levels through Butler, Armstrong and Clarion counties.

A map and profile of a line of levels along Slippery Rock creek.

CHAPTER I.

THE HISTORY OF PETROLEUM IN PENNSYLVANIA.

Section 1.—*The Rise and Progress of American Oil Mining—Theories of its Source—Improvident Manner of Working.*

The history of Petroleum is so much a matter of tradition and so familiar to all, that in presenting even an outline of such facts as it might seem important to record as reliable, the double difficulty is encountered, not only of rehearsing well worn statements, but also that of displacing and brushing away many errors, fancies and misconceptions that from the peculiar circumstances attending the excitement of its rapid and astonishing development, have grown from constant repetition to be considered as positive truth.

Regardless of either of these probable objections, it would seem eminently proper to place upon record here all such details as are known to be without question, and as fully as the limits of this paper will permit, for the purpose of forming a correct general estimate of what has been done in the past, what is the present situation, and what the promise of the future.

The earliest mention of Petroleum in the State of Pennsylvania seems to have occurred in the report of the Commander of Fort Duquesne to General Montcalm, in the year 1750, he having witnessed a ceremony of the Seneca Indians on Oil Creek, a prominent feature of which was a fire made from the oil which had oozed to the surface of the ground. Subsequently along the entire range, from New York to Tennessee, in which Petroleum has since been found, the earliest settlers, as well as the Indians, have not only found oil springs, or surface exudations of oil, but seem to have developed them in a crude way on account of the medicinal properties of the oil.

We find along Oil Creek, particularly between Titusville and Oil City, the circular, square and oval walled pits, from fifteen to twenty feet deep, cribbed with timber, which are so often referred to as being the work of a race of people who occupied the country prior to the advent of the Indian tribes. From the number of these pits and their systematic arrangement, Petroleum was doubtless obtained in considerable quantities. Trees of a growth of centuries have been found starting from within these pits, and their age correspondingly estimated; nevertheless, however we may be disinclined to disturb a story so interesting, it is perhaps equally possible that the pits spoken of being shallow, were walled around the tree, as the roots of a tree are often found to form a conduit for any fluid that is reaching the surface of the ground.

For many years the entire supply of "Naphtha," as it was commonly called, was obtained from the surface of these oil springs; sometimes by the use of a blanket or woolen cloth, which, when spread upon the surface, absorbed the surface oil, which was readily wrung out, and sometimes by the use of a few rude trenches, which conveyed the water and oil into a common basin, from which they were pumped into broad, shallow troughs, shelving off to the ground; where the water passed from each trough into the next a small skimmer was adjusted just under the surface of the water, so as to collect the oil and throw it off to one side.

As late as the year 1859 all the oil known as Seneca oil or naphtha was obtained in this way; small quantities were kept by chemists, and as a drug it was considered valuable for rheumatism, flesh-wounds and similar ailments.

Before leaving the earlier history of Petroleum, it may not be amiss to refer to the nation or people who held sway over these lands before the advent of the white man. They have left truly but few monuments or records, but to those who have passed much of their lives in the woods there is undisputed evidence that, as a race, they are to-day much under-valued. We think of them as Indians only, and our uppermost idea of an Indian is the low brute that has been retreating for two centuries from the Atlantic coast, before the advancing line of civilization.

But these were Indians, pure and uncorrupted; before many a log fire at night old settlers have recited how clear, distinct and immutable were their laws and customs; that when fully understood, a white man could transact the most important business with as much safety as he can to-day in any commercial centre.

One example may be valuable: We pride ourselves upon our railroads and telegraph as means of rapid communication, and yet while it was well known to the early settlers that news and light freight would travel with incomprehensible speed from tribe to tribe, people of the present day fail to understand the complete system by which this was done.

While running an old boundary line a few years ago the writer struck some blazes on the line trees which led off suddenly to the left. As they were in a totally different direction from that expected, the tree was blocked, and cutting out the mark, split the block down in the usual way to find the date of the blaze by counting the rings. The blaze was near the heart of the tree; a fortunate blow of the axe laid bare the dull, curled chip which was made by the stone hatchet of the Indian many years ago, and he knew then that he was on the old Indian trail from Fort Venango to Conewango Creek. These trails were "bee lines" over hill and dale, from point to point; here and there were open spots on the summits, where runners signaled their coming by fires when on urgent business, and were promptly met at stated places by fresh men.

In many places through the western counties, you will find traces of pits, that old residents will tell you were dug by white men hunting for silver, which, as well as copper, was common among the Indians and was supposed by first comers to be found in the vicinity; but as experience soon proved, the copper came perhaps, from Lake Superior by this Indian express, and the silver just as possibly from the far west. Our railroads wind along the valleys almost regardless of length or circuit, if a gradual rise can only be attained. To travellers on wheels, straight distances between points are much less formidable than is generally supposed. We find traces of the example of the Indian in the first white men; the first settlers above Titusville, on Oil Creek in 1809, took their bags of grain on their backs, walked to Erie, fifty-three miles to mill, and brought home their flour in the same way; the lumbermen at Warren and on the Brokenstraw, as related in the address of Judge Johnson to the old settlers of Warren county, rafted their lumber to New Orleans, and *walked home.*

This digression is made because it seems important to a comprehension of the earlier history of this product, to recognize fully the intelligence of the Indian, and also that if found on Oil Creek or in Virginia, there was no bar to its transportation throughout the entire range of connected tribes in all parts of the country.

The precursor of the discovery of Petroleum was that of salt; the woodsman found that the deer frequented certain springs, and that they were salt springs or deer-licks, so that he built his blinds and coverts in the trees overhead and in the brush around, with loop-holes for his gun, and shot his game at leisure.

Gradually from increased demand, the salt became valuable and the deer extinct. Pits were dug, and finally artesian wells were bored, many years before such wells were drilled for oil.

Tarentum, above Pittsburg, where the first salt wells were located, and probably the first place in which salt was produced for market in Western Pennsylvania, has since been a leading point in the manufacture of that article. Here, with the brine, was found a brown thick naphtha, which outside of its use as fuel in the evaporation, had always been a source of annoyance, and where found in considerable quantities, as was often the case in wells drilled for salt on the Upper Allegheny, occasioned the abandonment of the well.

The success of Mr. James Young, of Scotland, in the manufacture of illuminating oils from the destructive distillation of bituminous shale, stimulated the application of a similar process to the crude oil, and in 1850, Mr. Samuel Kier, of Pittsburg, erected a small refinery and commenced its distillation; his success was limited only to the small quantity which he was then enabled to obtain, and as the natural result of such a fact penetrating the minds of business men, the effort to remedy this was not long wanting.

The best known and the most prolific of the Oil Springs being on Oil Creek, Venango County, Pennsylvania, it was natural that the search for oil should first be there directed, and in 1858, Messrs. J. G. Eveleth and George H. Bissell, of New York City, having leased from Messrs. Brewer, Watson & Co., of Titusville, one hundred acres of land on the northern border of Venango County, just below the village, on which was an oil spring of considerable size, which had for years been the source of some small profit, they determined to sink upon it an artesian well, similar to those that were bored for salt at Tarentum and elsewhere.

For this purpose they engaged Mr. E. L. Drake, of New Haven, Connecticut, who seems to have had, as a sole recommendation, that quiet patience and perseverance which doggedly pursues its object unmoved by present difficulties, or the prospective results of future success or failure. His mission on earth, however, seems to have been accomplished by the sinking of this first well for oil, so much so, that he appears to have dropped out of sight soon afterward, as far as oil was concerned. It was not, however, for want of either ability or courage that he should do so, but perhaps awed by the flood of industry and commerce that, swelling with each successive year, has poured a stream of wealth from our State—by his first small rift in the rock—he felt that his work was complete; and the careful observer will, no doubt, fully concur in the belief that the testimonial of the State of Pennsylvania, in recognition of his services, was an act of simple justice, well deserved, to a man whose fame was well earned.

On Saturday afternoon, August 28, 1859, the drill of the Drake well dropped into the first crevice, at a depth of 71 feet; when the pump was adjusted, the well produced about twenty-five barrels per day, and the question of supply being virtually settled, a great industry was born.

From that time forward, at every surface indication on the bottom lands of the creeks, and along the Allegheny river, wells were rapidly put down. A second sand-rock was found underneath the first sand-rock of the Drake well, at a depth of about two hundred feet, which gave a greater yield, and in February, 1861, Mr. Funk found, upon the M'Elheny farm on Oil Creek, a third sand-rock, and the first flowing well, at a depth of 400 feet.

Soon afterwards the Phillips well, on the Tarr farm, Oil Creek, at the same depth, flowed three thousand barrels per day; and soon after that the Empire well, in the vicinity of Mr. Funk's first well, also three thousand barrels per day.

The consumption of oil at this time, as an illuminator, was, of course, not equal to this enormous supply, which was sold, for the time, at ten cents per barrel, and often given away, or let run to waste.

Production was paralyzed, and all small wells abandoned, and did not recuperate until 1864, when the total amount produced had declined to less than 4,000 barrels per day, and the demand, from the steadily increasing consumption, had made the highest market price yet known for Crude, of fourteen dollars per barrel maximum, and an average of over nine dollars for the year.

This increased demand was met by the developments at Pithole, and the discovery that the oil sand-rock was not indicated by, nor confined to the route of the water courses, but extended horizontally under the hills, and could be reached by the drill at a depth as much greater as the height of the hill required.

Bennehoff, Pioneer and Stevenson hills were thus developed in 1866; Tidioute and Triumph hills in 1867, and Pleasantville and Shamburg in 1868.

Production and demand ran almost side by side for the next two years. Search, however, was being made with untiring diligence for new oil producing spots.

There was little scientific record upon which to base calculation. Scientists, generally, were averse to giving opinions, without such a thorough investigation as would require not only money, but time, which the impatience of the operator could not spare, he therefore plunged into his work, trusting to give him a fair average of success, or perhaps to deluge him with favor—circumstances which, all combined, made the life of the producer, in the earlier times, one of the most intense excitement.

Theories, however, were not wanting; publications without number grappled with the subject and settled it to their own satisfaction for the time; among other suppositions of the origin of Petroleum was gravely stated, that it was the "urine of whales" from the North Pole, conveyed by subterranean channel. The term "Oil Belt," naturally fascinating, came early into use; maps were made showing the supposed course of the basin or underground river, containing of course, the grain of truth to the pound of error. The most valuable of all these propositions was that made by Mr. C. D. Angell, of Franklin, Pa., who, observing in 1871, that a number of the oil producing spots when noted upon a map, would be intersected by a straight line, whose bearing was about north sixteen degrees east, proceeded to define this line carefully upon the ground, and while he discovered at intervals upon it some new producing spots, yet failed to establish the theory advanced of continuous oil-belts.

As subsequent investigation has proved, the truth of his suggestion lay in the fact, that the general course of the grand current which deposited the sand-rock was in the direction named; the error of his statement, in the fact that nature never works with absolutely straight lines, and that the beds of sand-rock are deposited at intervals only, as may be seen to a greater or less extent in the bottom of any running stream. The course of the great belt of the Butler and Clarion region, generally north twenty-two degrees east, lies considerably east of Angell's first belt, and is crossed by a bed of sand-rock known as the "Fourth Sand," which was probably deposited by a previous cross-current in an entirely different direction.

The section of the oil country known as the Lower Oil Region, and comprising the territory south of Franklin, came first into notice in the year 1868, when the discovery of the position of the sand-rock equally under hill and valley, resulted in some good wells at Lawrenceburg, on the hill just above Parker's Landing.

Acting upon the discovery previously made of the general north-east and south-west direction of the sand-rock, its precise location was gradually defined by actual test, until the strip of oil producing territory had reached a length of over twenty miles, as shown on map B, and the published map, and extended from a point near the head-waters of Beaver Creek, in Clarion County, through Petersburg and Parker's Landing, to a point six miles south-west of Millerstown, in Butler County. The direction of the strip, is however, by no means a straight line as is popularly supposed, there being a bend at Parker's Landing, as shown, of from five to ten degrees.

It would be unnatural for any formation which was the result of a deposit from moving water, to be found in a perfectly straight line; in fact, if the centre of the development is carefully noted, it will be found to assume the form of a very slight wave or reversed curve.

For the past two years, 1873 and 1874, the production of oil has increased so rapidly that even the steady growing consumption, which has from its decrease in cost attained unexpected proportions, failed to maintain the balance essential to a healthful condition of the trade.

The result has been, that the production was necessarily confined to the largest wells, or rather that such new territory only was developed, as was expected to produce great results; development in the upper region, where the wells were of a moderate size, was gradually abandoned, and small wells shut down entirely, as the price received would not repay the cost of pumping.

Notwithstanding this, the surplus of oil steadily accumulated; the tankage of the oil region and the east was increased, until the amount now on hand, in the former place, amounts to over 3,100,000 barrels.

In 1873, when the enormous production first showed the signs of waning, an operator at Karns City, sinking an abandoned well deeper, struck a fourth sand-rock lying apparently seventy feet below the third, and obtained a well of 400 barrels.

Tracing out this rock, by development in the usual way, it was defined as a strip (shown on the published map, and map B) lying diagonally across the main belt, and extending for about eight miles from the head of Armstrong Run to Greece City, and is more fully described in the description of the section on map B.

The terminus of this cross-belt was found, for the present at least, at this latter point, a crescent of wells having been drilled to the south and west of it without result.

At the present time we are on the eve of another lull in the production, which may tend to improve the prospects of all interested. A continuation of the upper belt, however, when once discovered, will undoubtedly be followed up as unremittingly as before, and with equal disregard of the future.

Without considering the question of blame, or possibility of a remedy, it seems to be a fact that merits serious attention, that we have reaped this fine harvest of mineral wealth in a most reckless and wasteful manner.

When we carefully consider the short life of the best territory that has been found, how comparatively small is the relative proportion of the actual producing area to the entire region, it becomes a serious question, even in the face of the enormous production of to-day, whether we shall, in this Commonwealth, continue to supply petroleum to the next generation.

The prime difficulty encountered in operating the country in Kentucky and Tennessee, seems to have been only the distance from a market and want of proper facilities, all of which would be overcome by an increase in the price of the crude product.

Whether any protection to our general interests in this matter as a State is possible or advisable, is a question that present abundance has caused to be put out of sight.

Should American and even foreign Petroleum cease to be obtained, the world would be amply supplied with Shale oil.

It should however be remembered, that to take the lead in this matter, we should not only be able to produce oil, but to produce it the cheapest. Oil from twenty-five cents a barrel in 1861, rose to fourteen dollars a barrel in 1864. Should such a demand occur again, it is doubtful if operators would be content to glean the present fields, if fresh territory were to be found elsewhere.

One of the immediate causes of the rapid decline of oil territory is the "water logging" of the lower sand-rock. With the present system of casing a well and working through the casing, this evil has been remedied to a considerable degree.

The surface water of the upper sand-rocks seems in all cases to have been impenetrably sealed by the underlying slate from the oil bearing rocks below; in all territory, however, after the "head of gas" is taken off and the well ceases to flow from having expended its motive force, more or less surface water reaches the oil rock.

We are accustomed to consider water as a fluid of lighter gravity than any other with which we are practically acquainted, but in this case water is heavier than oil, and will fill the interstices of the rock to the exclusion of the oil. As this rock or sponge is simply the only reservoir from which we obtain oil, when it is water-logged our well is effectually "corked."

Were it possible to exclude from the sand-rocks every particle of water, we know from instances in isolated places, where the wells were fully controlled, that the production has not only continued for a number of years, but might seemingly with care have been prolonged many more.

It is also a question worthy of examination whether the production of the hill districts was not caused, or at least greatly increased, by the circumstances of the oil being driven back from the sands of the creek by this surface water.

Still another subject worthy of notice claims our attention and gives rise to the inquiry whether we are reaping, as a State and nation, any moderate share of the value of this product.

Refined oil retails in Great Britain at 45 cents per gallon; in Germany at 30 cents; in Austria about 40 cents; in Sweden and Norway at 66 cents per gallon, and at Melbourne, Australia, and other remote places at a still higher rate, so that refined oil costs the foreign consumer from fifteen to thirty dollars per barrel.

Furthermore, from the custom in vogue in Europe, of making mercantile contracts for a long term of years, the prices to the consumer do not at once follow the variations in the cost of raw material, but change more gradually.

As the foreign demand constitutes nearly three-fourths of the consumption, and as the cost of refining does not exceed two dollars per barrel, and the freight to Liverpool, five shillings or $1 25 per barrel, the question arises to what extent it is a matter of moment to the small dealer or the consumer abroad, whether oil at the wells can be purchased at fifty cents or five dollars per barrel, and consequently whether the income to the State and the oil community is fifteen thousand or one hundred thousand dollars per day.

As the case stands now, we are producing in reckless haste, at a positive loss to the community at large, regardless of the consequences to the territory itself or anything else, save the present bountiful supply. Whether a remedy exists, has become an open question; the chance and uncertainty attending the operations in the region, have rendered it impossible so far to establish any measures for mutual benefit.

Section 2.—Foreign Oil Fields.

It is only in the United States that artesian boring is resorted to for the purpose of obtaining oil in quantities. But at a number of points on the earth's surface there are surface indications of Petroleum which, in some instances, yield with the rudest machinery a considerable return.

The predominance of the American oil is due partly to its superior quality and partly to the abundance of its supply. Had labor and enterprise in other lands been as untrammeled as with us, we should not have enjoyed the present monopoly.

As it is, the supply is not only considerable, but, stimulated by our success, is slowly increasing, as the knowledge of our method becomes more widespread, and sooner or later will attain proportions that will interest us.

The prominent foreign oil fields existing to-day (not including, of course, the Canada region) may be stated as follows:

India.—The Rangoon district of the Burman Empire, on the Irawaddy river, which has produced oil for an unknown period, yielding from surface wells alone, by the latest and best authorities, nearly one million barrels per annum.

These wells are from fifty to two hundred and twenty feet in depth, of no greater sectional area than will permit a man to stand and work, and are cribbed or walled up with timber. (It is worthy of remark here that with all our modern appliances, we have been unable in this country to sink a shaft to that depth on account of the gas, which cannot fail to be present also in the Rangoon wells.) The oil and water being drawn to the surface by means of a bucket and windlass, and the oil being drawn off the top, is transported to market on ox-carts in earthen jars.

This oil, which, from all accounts, must be very similar to our "heavy oil," and does not command at the wells over fourteen cents per cwt., or about forty cents per barrel—a sum less than our own oil brings even in the present depression.

The British government, with an earnest desire to discover so valuable an article within the limits of its empire, has caused an examination to be made, by an American geologist, of the province of the Punjab, in British India, in the hope that a similar oil field might be obtained, but the result of the investigation was discouraging.

The difficulties attending any work in this climate on account of the excessive heat, allows but a few months of the year for active labor. The distance of the Punjab from the commercial centres of India, and the great expense of white labor employed there, will delay any great competition in this quarter.

An oil field is suspected to exist in the Province of Assam; but no investigation has yet been made, on account of the unwholesome and dangerous character of the region.

The following extract from the report of Mr. B. S. Lyman, the Geologist referred to, will give a synopsis of the "Punjab district:"

"In every case the oil seems to come from a deposit of very small horizontal extent, sometimes only a few feet, seldom as much as a few hundred yards. The oil comes from a thickness of about one hundred feet, and the natural springs yield, at one place, as much as *three quarts per day*, at all the *other* places the oil comes from a much smaller thickness of rock, from forty feet at Alugged, and twenty at Gunda and Punnoba, downward.

"The oil is dark green in color, and so heavy as to mark 25° of Beaume's scale or even less. The Gunda oil has been burned a little by the natives, with a simple wick resting on the side of an open dish, but the Punnoba oil is more inflammable, and needs a special tube for the wick."

An analysis of the Rangoon Naphtha specific gravity, 870; 100 parts gave tar 80 parts, burning oil 20 parts.

China.—There is a singular anomaly in the fact that American Petroleum is exported to China, in the face of the existence of the article and its production to some extent in some of the Provinces; to cap the climax, of what to an American would appear an absurdity, the Chinese have drilled artesian wells for the last century, attaining a depth of 2,000 feet. China, however, being such a chronic exception to all average human experience, we need not make any serious estimate of its future oil production.

Japan, likewise, has some prospects of oil which were being investigated by English capital, but as yet is only in the primary stages of development.

New Zealand.—Certain surface indications in the vicinity of Saranaki seem to indicate the promise of a future yield, which has not yet been realized to any great extent, although tools and proper implements were sent out from America, and a boring attained the depth of 375 feet.

Russia.—The Petroleum of the "Caucasus," on the shore of the Caspian Sea, obtained from the skimming of surface wells, has been known almost beyond the memory of man; the oil appears to vary in gravity from 28° to 38° Beaume, and until recently, had not been produced to any greater extent than one hundred thousand barrels per annum. American skill and machinery has nevertheless been employed the past two years, and with great success, oil having been found in great abundance at depths of less than two hundred feet.

Alsace and Hanover, in Europe; Peru and Ecuador, in South America, and Nova Scotia, in North America, have all produced a small amount of oil, and have all been operated by American enterprise, or by the aid of the knowledge gleaned from the work in Pennsylvania.

As an instance of the work that is being done in the outside oil fields, and with the object of throwing some light upon the idea that we are the sole and permanent possessors of this mineral wealth, the following extract from the letter of a friend residing in the oil regions of Gallacia, Austria, will give an inside view:

"LIBRANTOWA, *April* 28, 1874.

* * * * "A Chief Engineer of the Austrian government left me but an hour ago, who was sent to make an investigation of the Gallacian Oil Region, concerning the quantity and quality of oil produced; also to gather such information as could be obtained from the records of wells, with a view of locating a number of wells for the government to test the geological formation, and report the same to the Austrian Congress, (Reichrath,) now in session, to act upon, so as to enable the government to issue a geological map of the oil country.

"I may say that the geological formation here differs vastly from that of America, nothing but the tertiary alluvial formation has been found as yet, and the oil belts are, one and all, of anticlinal nature. * * * *

"But, nevertheless, oil has been produced in wonderful quantities, and in the most absurd and primitive way. If an American operator were to look upon one of these oil districts, he would, perhaps, form the idea that ground-hogs of immense size had been at work there, and yet when one looks at it closer and studies it deeper, it proves all the more the richness of the territory.

"Many of these holes have given a beggarly owner a princely return, some to the amount of $60,000 to $80,000 each—a large sum in this country—and if taken into consideration with the means with which the work was conducted, it certainly proves a rich remuneration.

"Within the last year the production has more than tripled from that of previous times, not exactly from more working, but from a better knowledge of local spots; whereas formerly there was more "wild catting."

"On the whole we have here now, at present, what you have had in America for some time past, and that is lots of oil and few buyers.

"The refineries here are, with a few exceptions, owned by Jews. Crude oil has always brought a price of from 6 to 7 florins per cwt., when refined oil was noted at 11 @ 12 florins per cwt., but now the price is but 4 @ 4½ per cwt., with oil at 12 florins at Vienna."

The figures given above would make "crude, at the wells," in Austria, 14 cents per gallon; in Pennsylvania, with the increased value of labor, the price is 1¼ cents.

CHAPTER II.

THE GEOGRAPHY OF PETROLEUM.

Section 1.—*General Description of the entire Oil Producing Range east of the Mississippi, as defined on Map A, including Canada, Pennsylvania, Ohio, West Virginia, Kentucky and Tennessee.*—(*See Map A.*)

The present watershed of the country through which passes the eastern range of oil production from New York to Tennessee, is that defined by the Ohio and Allegheny rivers, and the shores of Lake Erie.

The summit between the Allegheny river and the Lake lies much nearer to the Lake than is generally supposed, and is indicated by the contour line on Map A.

It will be seen that this summit approaches the Lake nearest at Chautauqua Lake, New York, where the "divide" between the Gulf of Mexico and Lake Erie is less than five miles from its shore.

Upon Map A is defined the relative position of all the territory east of the Mississippi, from which oil is now or has been furnished, including Canada, Ohio, West Virginia, Kentucky and Tennessee.

While of late years these other oil districts have for the time been overshadowed, as it were, and paralyzed by the enormous production of our own State, it is still advisable not to forget their existence, nor the probability that any cessation of supply on our part, would cause such a direction of enterprise and capital to their heretofore poorly worked fields, as might result in very serious competition.

Furthermore, it is convenient for geographical reference, to note that all the oil found in the eastern United States, is contained in a belt or range parallel with, and considerably west of, the Allegheny Mountains.

The four separate oil regions differ from each other so materially in almost every particular, that an accurate conception of the relative value of our own section would not be obtained by the general observer, without noting the special characteristics of the other three.

The Canada Oil Regions.

The Canada Oil Regions are situated in the western part of the Dominion, in the counties of Lambton, Bothwell and Kent, Province of Ontario. They extend from near Lake Erie to Lake Huron, and from the St. Clair river eastward about seventy miles.

The prominent oil producing points are Petrolia, Lambton county, Oil Springs, Bothwell county, and Bothwell, Kent county.

Petrolia is sixteen miles south-east of the outlet of Lake Huron; Oil Springs seven miles south of it, and Bothwell thirty-five miles from Oil Springs.

Western Canada has no coal, the land descends gently to the south-west, and the general dip of the rock is westerly.

The oil of Canada is found in a flint-bearing limestone, varying from close to open in its construction, and largely composed of marine shells, and other fossils peculiar to that geological horizon, the "Corniferous Limestone."

The gravity of the oil is from 33° to 43° Beaume.

The following record of the wells near Petrolia, indicates the special difference of the underlying rock:

Yellow clay, 5 to 15 feet.

Compact blue clay, 50 to 100 feet, resting on a thin shell of limestone resembling stalactite.

A gravel bed, 2 to 8 feet.

Slate, (Hamilton) 15 feet.

Corniferous Limestone, 40 feet, surface wells found here.

Slate, 30 feet.

Limestone, 40 feet.

Slate, 3C feet.

Corniferous Limestone, 250 feet; all the oil found in this horizon.

Hard blue sandstone, 4 feet; underneath this a vein of salt water, apparently inexhaustible.

At this point commences the "Onondago Salt Group," (a formation of unknown thickness here,) in which is found the salt of

Syracuse, and also of Goderich, on Lake Huron. It has been penetrated at Petrolia, in several places, to the depth of five hundred feet without producing a barrel of oil.

The entire production of the Canada Oil Region, at present, does not exceed 2,500 barrels per day.

The Pennsylvania Oil Region.

Two lines drawn through the extreme eastern and western limits of all known developments to this date, are shown on Map B, and marked as the eastern and western dividing lines between the oil and the gas wells. These lines are taken solely for the object of giving some shape and definite locality to what is generally known as the "Oil Region," and include everything that has at present a claim to such a title.

They embrace a narrow strip of territory extending into Cattaraugus county, New York, and a broad area reaching over slightly into Ohio, the southern edge of which is not yet fully defined.

The Oil Regions of Ohio and West Virginia..

These Oil Regions are confined to two plainly marked belts of geological disturbance, (anticlinal,) shown on Maps A and B; one extending from Newport, Ohio, north through Washington and Morgan counties, and southward, in West Virginia, about forty miles through Ritchie, Wood and Wirt counties, and embracing the producing localities of Horse-neck, Sand-Hill, Volcano, (the principal point,) White Oak and Burning Springs, and a smaller belt a few miles to the west of it.

The minimum width of the belt is about two and a half miles, and the point of greatest upheaval is at White Oaks, at which place the strata, forming the western border of the break, are inclined at an angle of 60°; at Oil Rock and Burning Springs, the inclination is about 20°.

The special peculiarities of this region may be stated as follows:

Oil is found in crevices at a certain fluid level, without the slightest regard to the character of the rock in which the crevice may exist. Where a natural crevice has not been reached by the drill, the use of the torpedo seldom fails to open connection with one.

No surface water is found in the wells, and often no salt water. At Volcano, especially, the oil is pumped clear, with a very slow motion of the walking beam not exceeding twenty strokes per minute.

The oil ranges between 28° and 40° Baume, and wells of all gravities of oil are found indiscriminately side by side.

While the character of the underlying rocks of West Virginia and Ohio is a matter of no value, so far as the indication of oil is concerned, the following record of the wells at Volcaco, West Virginia, which is the greatest producing point, may be of some interest:

Conductor, or pipe to rock, - - - - - -	5 feet.
Yellow sand, - - - - - - - - -	45 "
Shale, - - - - - - - - - -	20 "
Hard fine sand, - - - - - - -	14 "
White shale, - - - - - - - - -	23 "
Dark sand, - - - - - - - - -	28 "
Shale, - - - - - - - - - -	60 "
Gray and soft sand, - - - - - - -	66 "
Shale, - - - - - - - - - -	47 "
Sand, - - - - - - - - - -	14 "
White sand, (Surface water lost here,) - - -	66 "
Soft shelly sand, (show of oil,) - - - -	22 "
Gray sand, - - - - - - - - -	21 "
Dark coarse sand, - - - - - - - -	31 "
White sand and pebble, - - - - - -	19 "
Sand-rock, - - - - - - - - -	4 "
Total, - - - - - - - - -	485 "

The total production of the entire region, at present, does not exceed five hundred barrels per day.

Kentucky and Tennessee.

Had it been ordered that the Ohio river should flow eastward, instead of West and South, it is probable that Kentucky and Tennessee would, to-day, share with Pennsylvania in the supply of petroleum to commerce.

All that we know at present, reliably, about this section, is, that it has produced, from surface wells, enormous quantities of oil.

A well on Crocus creek, in Cumberland county, Kentucky, at a depth of 191 feet produced, for a time, 300 barrels per day. The wells on Boyd's creek, Barren county, near Glasgow; the oil springs beginning on the Cumberland river, and stretching through north-west Kentucky, and the wells in Overton county, Tennessee, seem to indicate the probability of a large production, if thoroughly developed.

The fact, however, of the presence of sulphur in the oil, the distance of the territory from the great eastern centres, the expense of transportation over a difficult route, and the ample resources of Pennsylvania, have completely held back operations on a scale of any magnitude.

THE PENNSYLVANIA OIL REGION.

Section 2.—*Description of the Pennsylvania Oil Region proper, as contained within the lines drawn between the Oil and the Gas wells, with reference to the known oil areas and oil centres as defined on Map B and the published Map.*

In the following description of the separate localities in which oil has been found in Pennsylvania, those places which are well known are referred to under their particular names; the outlying and intermediate points, surrounding and connecting the great oil producing areas, are numbered on Map B, from 1 to 65, and mentioned in numerical order in the next section.

Tidioute.

The extreme north-western terminus of the Pennsylvania Oil Region is the district of Tidioute and vicinity, on the Allegheny river, in Deerfield township, Warren county; it comprises the New York and Allegheny, the Tidioute and Warren, the Wallace, Boyne, Cleland, Triumph, Grove, Hallen and Dennis Run tracts. On the opposite side of the river the Economy society have a tract of twelve thousand acres, upon which is located an oil area of considerable extent.

The first wells of Tidioute, (among the earliest in the region,) were located upon the banks and islands of the river, and found no small quantities of oil at depths of one hundred and one hundred and fifty feet.

Subsequent operations showed the existence of this sand-rock under the hills on either side, from which the best wells were obtained.

Triumph City is located on the hill west of Tidioute, at a height of 592 feet above the river, and was the centre of the most successful operations in 1869 and 1870.

The first well in Warren county was located on Gorman run, one mile from the river; it was two and a half inches in diameter and sixty-three feet deep. Owing to the fact that the oil sand-rock was found so near the surface on the river, a shaft of seven by nine feet in section was commenced on the river bank in 1865, by the New York Enterprise Mining Company, and sunk to a depth of 160 feet, entering the third sand-rock as much as thirty feet.

A large amount of the rock was removed and brought to the surface, and was found to be an open porous conglomerate of small pebbles and a cementing matter of alumina and silica; it was rather friable when long exposed to the air, and capable of holding a large amount of oil.

A fatal accident, caused by an explosion of the accumulated gas, terminated all work on the undertaking.

A well on the island at Tidioute, drilled to the depth of 1,000 feet, failed to find any sand below 125 feet from the surface.

The best wells at Tidioute and Triumph Hill have reached 400 barrels per day, and the thickness of the sand is not fully known, as operators were careful not to pierce it, but went only 50 or 60 feet in the rock.

The wells on the hill-land of the Economy tract opposite Tidioute, are worthy of a special examination; the oil found in these wells came from a horizon above the river level, a totally exceptional case in all the annals of the oil region, and one which is so well established as not to permit of any doubt.

West Hickory.

West Hickory is an oil area directly south of Tidioute, comprising the Fagundas, Tuttle, Beatty, Scott and other farms.

A small amount of heavy oil of 27°, not exceeding 12 or 15 barrels per well, was produced on West Hickory creek, a short distance above its mouth, on the White farm, at a depth of 400 feet. After this development had ceased, the inevitable search in the north-west direction, resulted in the Venture well on the Fagundas farm, which at a depth of 750 feet, found a third sand of 55 feet in thickness. The territory of West Hickory was defined from this well, and in consideration of its size, has produced an unprecedented amount of oil, from a well of 400 barrels maximum. Pipe lines from West Hickory lead to Titusville, and to Garland on the Philadelphia and Erie railroad.

New London.

New London is the connecting link between Tidioute and Colorado, and lies just west of Tidioute. It comprises the land of the New London Petroleum Company and the adjacent farms, and while none of the wells are very large, the production has been steady and uniform. The thickness of the sand-rock is from 40 to 55 feet, at a depth of about 650 feet.

Colorado.

Colorado, lying between Enterprise and New London, in Warren county, comprises the lands of Benson, Hopins & Co., Jay and others. The wells have been as large as one hundred and fifty barrels per day, and the sand-rock is found on the flat of a thickness of about forty feet, and at an average depth of 525 feet. From Enterprise to Tidioute, may be found through Colorado and New London, a complete line of wells centering however, at the points named.

This range of oil-rock is doubtless far from being fully determined, the overwhelming supply of the lower oil fields having put a stop to active developments for a time.

Enterprise.

Enterprise, a village four miles east of Titusville, on Pine creek, Warren county, has a few scattered wells, which have produced a small amount of oil for a long time, from a sand-rock 17 to 38 feet thick, found at a depth of about 450 feet.

As small wells have almost always been the "avant couriers" of larger ones, it would not be surprising if a larger area of good sand-rock were eventually found in this vicinity.

Titusville.

The prominence which the striking of the first well gave to Titusville, added to the advantages of its site, has been so far fully maintained by the enterprise and public spirit of its citizens. With pavements, sewers, gas, a splendid system of water works, and ample and elegant schools, all acquired at a moderate cost, together with churches of all prominent denominations, it is unquestionably a desirable place of residence. The Oil Districts around Titusville, are—

The Watson Flats, and the *Guild* and *Parker Flats*, at the junction of Oil and Pine creeks, which produced, together with the adjoining lands of Kingsland Oil Company and Original Petroleum Company, a great part of the oil from 1859 to 1864.

The *Drake Well* was located on Oil creek, on the land now owned by the Watson Petroleum Company, New York, a narrow strip extending across Oil creek, about a mile and a half below the town. The oil of the Drake well was found not in a sand-rock, but in a crevice; the well was subsequently drilled deeper and a first sand found at 150 feet, 10 feet thick; a second at 370 feet, 55 feet thick, and no third sand found at 480, or in other wells adjoining drilled to 550 feet. Within the city limits but little oil has been found, and none whatever of any moment on Oil creek north of it.

A well was drilled by Mr. Jonathan Watson, in the city, at the foot of the hills on the north side, to the depth of 2,114 feet, for the purpose of ascertaining the existence of any oil producing sand below that found on the creek. This work will undoubtedly prove of great value in further investigation of the strata, and is shown in the section on Map B.

Church Run is a separate oil area, north of Titusville, comprising the Cadwallader, Weed, Kerr, M'Guire, Atlantic and Great Western, Barnsdall and other farms; the sand-rock here does not seem to occupy quite the same geological horizon as that found on the flats below the city, a circumstance which subsequent examination may disprove or explain.

The wells on Church Run, while never exceeding 300 barrels, have produced a great deal of oil, and are very lasting; the sand-rock being from 60 to 75 feet in thickness, and found on the run at a depth of 480 feet.

The *Octave District*, comprising the Hyde, Curry and other farms, is a continuation of the sand-rock of Oil Creek below Titusville, in the usual course to the south-west. The wells are small but durable, and the general depression in oil matters has prevented the extent of this area from being fully defined.

The sand-rock is from fifty to seventy feet in thickness, and is found at a depth of about 875 feet.

Miller Farm is a shipping station of some importance, six miles south of Titusville, on Oil Creek, and is the location of a considerable amount of iron tankage.

Some oil was obtained in 1864, from shallow wells in the first sands, (possibly from a surface drainage from the wells north of it,) but the quantity was inconsiderable.

Pleasantville, an aptly named town in Venango county, lies at the head of the great stretch of sand-rock that terminates at Cherry-tree Run.

The land, in this vicinity, is too much sub-divided for general mention, the original owners being Brown Bros., Mitchell, Benedict, Dunham and others.

The highest point of land in Venango county, 1,762 feet above ocean level, lies just east of the town.

National Wells, on West Pit-hole creek, is the nucleus of a district lying within the great stretch just mentioned, and was a pioneer of operations in this section, having been struck in 1866; the third sand is found about fifteen feet thick, at a depth of 745 feet on the run.

The wells do not exceed thirty barrels, but from the extent of the rock, and the care exercised in pumping and drilling, the amount produced has been considerable.

West Pit-hole.—A small area of sand-rock under the Paxton, Keech, Hydrick and Turner farms, in Allegheny township, Venango county.

Wells on Paxton farm find the sand at 730 feet—fourteen feet thick.

Shamburg.

Shamburg, Oil Creek township, Venango county, a noted oil centre, now nearly exhausted, was first brought into notice by a well on Cherry run, on the land of the Pittsburg and Cherry Run Petroleum Company.

The prominent farms of Shamburg are the Atkinson, Tallman, Clark, Fleming, King, Dearborn, Bennehoff, Goss and Stowell.

The sand-rock, on the run, is found at a depth of 775 feet, and is from 60 to 75 feet thick.

While the largest wells of this section did not reach 500 barrels, there probably was no locality found which has contained so *many* good wells. The price of oil also, during the time of its development, was such as to bring a large return.

The following record of well No. 12, on the land of the Pittsburg company, is so minute and accurate as to possess an especial value.

38 feet of driving pipe.

At 38 feet, a soft slate rock.

At 70 feet, first sand-rock.

At 71 feet, water crevice.

At 91 to 112 feet, crevices.

At 130 feet, bottom of fine white sand-rock 60 feet thick.

At 132 feet, gray sand-rock bluish cast.

At 152 feet, bottom of same, 20 feet thick.

At 153 feet, slate rock, good drilling to 245 feet.

At 245 to 256 feet, hard dark slate and sand to 278 feet.

At 278 feet, hard pebble sand shell 18 inches thick.

At 280 to 289 feet, hard gray sand and slate.

At 289 feet, second sand-rock hard pebble, 11 feet thick.

At 300 feet, sand bluish cast, white pebbles, 5½ feet thick.

At 305½ feet, gray and white shells for 29½ feet.

At 338 to 440 feet, blue sandy rock, mixed with slate.

At 420 to 480 feet, blue and red rock alternate.

At 505 feet, hard blue rock shell 15 feet thick.

At 520 feet, third sand very hard, white and yellow pebbles, 10 feet thick.

At 530 feet, mud vein.

At 545 feet, through third sand 25 feet thick, two crevices and gas very strong.

At 545 to 575 feet, blue sand and slate to 605 feet.

At 608 feet, hard shell 2 feet thick.

At 610 to 636 feet, blue slate.

At 636 feet, hard white sand, mixed with pebble, hard shell, 4 to 5 feet thick.

At 640 feet, top of fourth sand.

At 648 to 654 feet, hard pebble.

At 654 feet, large gas vein and show of oil.

At 655 feet, bad mud vein.

At 668 feet, through fourth sand 28 feet 6 inches thick.

At 745 feet, slate, hard shell, 6 inches thick.

At 745 to 748, hard slate.

At 748 feet, hard shell, yellow pebble and good gas vein.

At 750 feet, slate rock.

At 768 feet, slate and hard shells.

At 776 feet, top of fifth sand.

At 776 to 778 feet, pebble rock, open and porous.

At 778 feet, crevice, gas vein and good show of oil.

At 781 feet, rock becomes darker.

At 783 feet, dark rock, gassy.

At 784 feet, porous rock.

At 792 feet, white and yellow pebble, crevice, oil and gas.

At 794 feet, white rock, coarse and porous.

At 806 feet, mud vein.

At 828 to 830 feet, white and yellow pebble.

At 830 feet, hard close white sand.

At 834 feet, slate and sand mixed.

At 835 feet, bottom of the well.

A marked peculiarity of the great stretch of oil-rock, of which Shamburg forms a part, and one which deserves future examination, is the existence of black and green oil, so called, side by side in the same territory, so that the surface line between the two classes of wells can be sharply defined.

Red Hot, a suburb of Shamburg, on the land of Independent Oil Company and vicinity, lies between Shamburg and the National wells. A stranger visiting the locality and traveling through the unbroken line of derricks from Shamburg to Pleasantville, would hardly be able to identify these separate places. The sand rock is simply an extension of that underlying Shamburg.

Pit-hole.

Pit-hole, Allegheny township, Venango county, comprises the territory on Pit-hole creek, included in the Holmden, Morey, Blackmer, Rorker, Hyner, Copeland, M'Kinney, Ball, Dawson, Blank and other farms.

The area of this sand-rock, although unusually prolific, was small in comparison with the beds lately discovered. The Frazier and Grant wells on the Holmden farm, flowing at the rate of 700 and 450 barrels per day, gave a great impetus to the development, and the price of oil at the time, furnished the means for so much extravagant expenditure, that it may be safely stated that no oil in the region was ever obtained at an equal cost. A city of ten thousand inhabitants, with all the concomitants of vice, luxury and piety, started into life in a few months and fading with the decline of the territory within a year, was so nearly obliterated by fire and bodily removal, that scarcely a vestige remains to-day. An example so striking and so extreme cannot probably be found elsewhere.

The sand-rock on the flats of Pit-hole creek, is here found at a depth of over 600 feet, and but from 14 to 20 feet thick.

Cash Up, a small sand-rock on the Huidekoper farm and the edges of adjoining tracts, about two miles north-east of Pit-hole. Although of not very great extent, it nevertheless was remarkable for its production; the first well, which was drilled to an upper sand-rock with a small production, being subsequently purchased by some old operators, who, on drilling deeper, obtained a well flowing 1,100 barrels per day.

Bean Farm, including the Golden farm and several smaller tracts, lies east of Pleasantville and north of Pit-hole, in Allegheny township, Venango county. The wells were small and proportionately lasting.

Bull Run and Cow Run, Oil Creek township, Venango county. The mouth of Bull run, which is a deep gorge from off Oil creek between two hills, is covered by the fifty acres of the Farel farm, upon which, at the mouth of the run, the famous Noble well flowed to the extent of 2,500 barrels per day; the Patterson farm and land of the Caldwell Oil Company span the balance of the run, and the land of the Clinton Oil Company likewise encloses Cow run adjacent to the north, nearly all of which is underlaid with a good producing sand-rock. The sand-rock is a continuation of the sand-rock of Oil creek.

Petroleum Centre.

The first success of any magnitude at this well known place, was upon the Hyde and Egbert farm, a triangular flat at the base of the M'Cray hill, which a few years afterwards was also successfully developed.

The Maple Shade and the Coquette wells are so familiar as to need no further mention than that their production was from 400 to 500 barrels per day.

The town itself is situated on the land of the Central Petroleum Company, a great part of which has been found productive. The Woods, Pearson, Claremont and other farms, extending over the hill to Cherrytree run, have all been found to overlie at 950 feet, a fine bed of oil sand-rock 45 feet thick, which, however, stops precipitately at the run.

Bennehoff run and hill, Pioneer run, the Upper and Lower M'Elheny farms and M'Cray hill, are all suburbs of the Centre, and have in their time been great producing localities. The sand-rock at the Centre, is found on the flats at a depth of 475 feet and is about 40 feet thick. On the adjacent hills, the depth is correspondingly increased.

Columbia Oil Company, (Story Farm.)

The *Story Farm* deserves special mention, not only for the success accorded to its development, but from the excellence of its management.

On 500 acres of land there have been drilled over 180 wells, producing nearly one millions barrels of oil, and paying dividends to the stockholders of the company to the amount of nearly three millions of dollars, over all expenses, within a period of less than ten years.

The territory is now exhausted, but the record of the work remains as a permanent example of what the careful management of oil territory can accomplish. The sand-rock here is found at 480 feet, and of the same thickness as at Petroleum Centre.

Blood, *Rynd* and *Tarr* farms, on Oil creek, between Petroleum Centre and Rouseville, are well known as land marks in the early stages of the oil excitement.

The famous Blood well of 1,000 barrels per day, and the Phillips well on the Tarr farm, which flowed by actual measurement, in twenty-four hours, 3,940 barrels, and produced over 500,000 barrels of oil, together with the Woodford and other wells indicated the richness of the underlying rock. The sand-rock is from 38 to 58 feet in thickness at the usual depth of Oil creek rock.

Rouseville.

Rouseville, an oil town formerly of over 3,500 inhabitants, is situated on Oil creek, at the mouth of Cherry run. The bed of sand-rock, which is almost continuous from Petroleum Centre to Oil City, extends up Cherry run for about two miles. The four Reed wells on the Criswell tract, located on a single acre, produced upwards of 100,000 barrels of oil; the most prominent of the farms on Cherry run above Rouseville are the Union Petroleum Company, the Mingo Oil Company, the Brevoort and the Smith farm. The third sand is from 27 to 42 feet in thickness, and is found at a depth of 550 feet, somewhat greater than Oil creek, on account of the rise of the run.

The *M'Clintock*, *Steele*, *Buchanan* and *Clapp* farms lie between Rouseville and Oil City, and have all been good producing farms, but are substantially described by those which have just preceded.

With a few lingering exceptions, the valley of Oil Creek, as an oil producing district, is rapidly becoming a thing of the past; its demise was, no doubt, accelerated by the transfer of capital and energy to the more prolific fields of Butler county. With many the belief is strong that future enterprise will clear out its water-logged sand-rocks, and find a fresh supply of the product, but at present many of its mushroom towns are totally obliterated; such buildings as were not destroyed by fire, have been carted bodily away. Waving grain and gardens occupy the richer flat land that teemed with the wild excitement of 1865, and cover the rusty nozzles of the driving pipes.

And yet when we remember that Oil creek, within this length of twenty miles, has produced over *one hundred and ten million* dollars worth of oil from an actual area of less than three square miles, mined with a most appalling waste, it is doubtful if any portion of the earth's surface has ever given to man an equal return for his labor.

Oil City.

Oil City, while possessing an admirable location which, in the future, as in the case of Pittsburg, may be the means of overcoming all present obstacles, still labors under natural disadvantages, so far as the expansion of the city is concerned. These have been met by her citizens with unusual courage, perseverance and liberality. The city long since surmounted the steep hills which enclose it, and crowned them with good streets and pleasant homes, and it has also included the town of Venango, upon the opposite side of the Allegheny river, consolidating the connection by means of two substantial bridges.

There seems to be two stages in the life of all mining towns; the first, when buildings of rough lumber are hastily thrown together on the surface of the ground, merely to accommodate present urgent need, and when the country depends, to use a forcible but homely expression, entirely "on greenbacks and ten-penny nails."

The second is, when the ravages of fire, a sure visitor of such places, are replaced with substantial buildings of stone, brick and iron. A town which survives the first stage, and passes into the second, possesses some certain elements of durability.

The substantial improvements of Oil City are all the more remarkable from the unusual natural difficulties with which it was necessary to contend. Along the creek, and the river flats on both sides, in the vicinity of Oil City, good fair producing wells have been found; the third sand having an average depth of about 475 feet, and being from 20 to 55 feet in thickness.

Stand Off City, or Shaw farm, lies between Oil City and Cherry Run, on the summit of the hill; the sand-rock being a continuation of that from the creek, andfrom 20 to 57 feet thick.

Charley Run and Shaffer Run are small streams entering the Allegheny, and the creek, within the limits of Oil City; from these two runs a stretch of sand-rock is found, extending over to Reno on the river.

Reno.

The town of Reno was a bold attempt on the part of Mr. C. V. Culver, to divert the trade of the upper Oil Region to a point on the Allegheny river possessing greater natural advantages than Oil City.

For this purpose a railroad was constructed, at an enormous expense, from Pit-hole to Reno over the hills; the town of Reno lying upon a beautiful slope on the north bank of the river, was built as its terminus, and furnished at once with a handsome station, hotel and all the improvements and facilities of a long established place.

That the enterprise miscarried is due, doubtless, more to the financial crash of 1865, than to any other cause.

The continuation of the sand-rock of Charley run, on the Reno lands, in 1867, has given some prosperity to the place. The sand-rock is found, on the river, at a depth of about 500 feet, and the territory being unusually well managed, has been proportionately lasting.

Walnut Bend, on the Allegheny river above Oil City, overlies a bed of sand-rock which was operated to some extent in 1865.

Sage Run, which empties into the Allegheny river opposite Oil City, is the commencement of a stretch of sand-rock which begins at a point on the run, one and a half miles from the river, and extends westward beyond the head of the run, over the hills of Cranberry township, Venango county, including the Sands, Schwartz and other farms, and terminating in an oil town of short life known as Bredinsburg, a few miles south-west of Oil City. The wells have produced as much as 300 barrels each per day, and the sand-rock is found from 900 to 1,100 feet from the surface, and from 18 to 20 feet in thickness.

The railway of the Cranberry Coal Company, whose extensive lands lie to the south-east of Oil City, and their coal on the summit of the hills, follows the general course of the run.

Franklin.

The wells of Franklin and Sugar creek, which, with the wells of Smith's ferry, Ohio, and Slippery Rock creek, Lawrence county,

Pennsylvania, mark the extreme north-western boundary of the actual producing district, find their oil in the uppermost oil-producing sand-rock on the great slope from the north-west.

Future investigation will perhaps connect this with the fact, that all three of these places produce heavy oil. The sand-rock is found at a depth of 260 feet, beneath the flat, is geologically higher than that of Oil City, and is from 50 to 80 feet in thickness. The gravity of the oil ranges from 30° to 32°, and the largest producing well has attained 150 barrels per day.

The territory extends over to Two Mile run, and includes the lands of George P. Smith, M'Calmont, Fee and others.

Franklin, the county seat of Venango county, (the site of old Fort Venango,) a substantial city of 7,000 inhabitants, is so interwoven with the earliest history of our State, that it needs no repetition here.

Foster, on the Allegheny river below Franklin, overlies a small detached bed of sand-rock, situated in the general sweep of the oil bearing areas north-east and south-west from Reno and Petroleum Centre. It comprises the Foster, Miller and Bonsall tracts, lying on both sides the river. The third sand is found at 610 feet, and is from 12 to 14 feet thick.

Bully Hill.—This territory was one of the discoveries attendant on the belt line of Mr. C. D. Angell, heretofore mentioned; it lies upon the hill between Franklin and Foster, and comprises the Stroman and other farms.

Scrub Grass, on the Allegheny river, opposite the mouth of Scrub Grass creek, is also an isolated territory over a small bed of sand-rock. The development here was the result of large purchases of land by the Philadelphia and Boston Petroleum Company. The producing area includes Belle island, the M'-Millen and other farms. The depth of the sand-rock on the river is 615 feet, and its thickness from 18 to 20 feet.

East Sandy.

East Sandy lies upon the extreme south-eastern edge of the present oil development, and is the only connecting link, at present, between the upper and lower oil fields. It comprises the land of East Sandy Lloyd Oil Company, Montgomery Oil

Company, and others, and is situated on East Sandy creek, in Rockland township, Venango county.

Gas City is the name of the settlement which forms the centre of operations, and takes its name from the great gas veins which occur in all the wells here. The sand-rock has a thickness of sixty feet, and is found at a depth of 850 feet.

The Burning well of East Sandy was situated in Pine Grove township, between main Sandy creek and the branches of the same, it was drilled in 1866 850 feet to the third sand, when a mud vein was found, and the tools stuck. The out-pouring of gas was so great, that from carelessness it soon took fire and burned a long time.

The Lower Oil Fields.

We come now to the great Lower Oil Belt, a term in this case not misapplied, beginning at Triangle City, on Beaver creek, Clarion county, and terminating for the present, at St. Joe, in Butler county, in length twenty-one miles.

It would seem desirable that any statement concerning this remarkable producing area, the greatest found so far, and in all probability the greatest that ever will be, that it should be made only after the fullest and most thorough collation of every detail of facts which can possibly bear upon it. But there will be no attempt made in this report, to go beyond the citation of such facts as are too well known to be questioned and are essential to explain the connection of the salient features of this region with the Upper Oil region, concerning which we have fuller information.

A sand-rock found at Brady's Bend in 1866, at the depth of 1,100 feet, with some oil, gave rise to a further investigation of the river above, and resulted in the discovery of a sand-rock of 57 feet, at a depth of 960 feet on the river at Parker's Landing in 1868. It was not until 1870 that the search for the limits of this sand-rock on the north-east and south-west line, extended it to the hills at Lawrenceburg, back of Parker's, and to the mouth of the Clarion river.

The bend in the belt as now defined, and which will be observed on the maps, caused no small amount of "wild catting," and some fortunate delay; the belt when once found however, was soon worked back to the starting point; owing to the height of the hills, a number of wells which were supposed to be failures, were afterwards drilled to the proper depth with great results. On the north-east, Petersburg, Antwerp, Turkey City and Beaver Creek, were successively embraced within the limits of the belt, and on the south-west, Petrolia, Karns City and Millerstown.

After leaving Karns City, the belt seems to divide into two well defined and separate beds, known as the East and West belts, one of which has been prolonged to St. Joe.

The entire width of this great stretch of rock does not exceed three miles, and to the fact of so vastly productive an area being found continuous, instead of in detached spots as in the Upper Region, the rapid development is due.

The sand-rock dips so rapidly after leaving Scrub Grass, that many of the wells of this section are as much as 1,600 feet in depth; if these are drilled without loss at the present prices of oil, we may safely set it down as a fact which will have no small bearing on the future, that the maximum depth at which a sand-rock can be profitably found, is yet an unknown quantity.

That part of the great belt lying east of the river, yielding the greater part of its production from wells of moderate size, has shared to some extent in the lull which the great spouters of Butler county brought upon the balance of the region. Should the price of oil appreciate or the production of the south end fall off, we may look for further operations in this direction.

Some idea of the relative position of the sand-rock along the belt from the upper end southward, may be obtained from the following data:

At Turkey City, sand on flat at 1,150, 20 feet thick.

Ocean Level of Pump Station, Turkey City, 1,179 feet.

St. Petersburg, Fountain well, 1,241 feet, 26 feet of sand.

Blanchard & Siggins' well, D. Ritt's farm, 1,063 feet, 26 feet of sand.

Eddinger farm, St. Petersburg, 1,150 feet, sand 24 feet.

Peter King farm, Ritchey run, 1,000 feet, 23 feet of sand.

Casino well, Parker's Landing, 1,065, 36 feet of sand.

Murray well, J. Marshall farm, Parker's, 1,027, 30 feet of sand.

Bear creek, above the mouth, 1,170 feet, 33 feet of sand.

Karns City, Ocean Level, 1,230 feet.

Third sand found at 1,440; fourth sand at 1,535.

Third sand, about 26 feet thick.

Modoc wells, 1,450, sand 12 to 15 feet thick.

William Moore farm, two miles south of Karns City, sand at 1,560 feet.

Armstrong run, near Brady's Bend, at 1,263 feet, 7½ feet in third sand.

Wells at Millerstown, average depth, 1,550 to sand.

On James M'Cready farm, three and a half miles south-west of Millerstown, 1,530 feet to sand.

Section 3.—*The Description of the Outlying Points that have been Tested, numbered on Map B from* 1 *to* 65.

Between the main beds of sand-rock which are the great centres of development, and to the north-west and south-east of the range of productive oil areas, there are isolated localities which have been explored to a greater or less extent and which are particularly valuable for completing our conception of the general situation of the oil bearing strata.

The most prominent of these are given below, simply with the expectation that they will serve as guides to point the way to further and closer investigation. They are numbered on Map B from 1 to 65, the description given containing only such portions of the information as could be obtained at present and deemed perfectly reliable.

No. 1. Heavy oil at a depth of 150 feet, near Lowell, Mahoning county, Ohio. Well afterwards sunk to a depth of 900 feet, and gas obtained, but no oil.

No. 2. Slippery Rock Creek, above Wurtemburg, Lawrence county, Pennsylvania; a number of good producing wells, some as large as fifty barrels, but not lasting, the oil was of heavy gravity.

No. 3. Oil Spring Reservation, Oil Creek, Allegheny county, New York; this locality has been long known for its surface oil.

No. 4. A well at Limestone, Cattaraugus county, New York, in March, 1872, produced for a short time some oil of 45° gravity; this well was 1,050 feet deep, had much gas, and yielded at first about five barrels per day.

No. 5. Wells on Cow run, near Marietta, Ohio. These wells are on the main belt of anticlinal in the Ohio oil region, and are about 450 feet in depth.

No. 6. Wells on Duck creek, Washington county, Ohio; a part of the same belt just mentioned.

No. 7. Well at Utica, French creek, Venango county; seven barrels per day of heavy oil.

No. 8. Gas well at Leechburg, on the Kiskeminitis river, seven miles above its mouth; this well is 1,200 feet deep, produces no oil, but an enormous amount of gas which is used as fuel by manufactories. The oil springs on the Kiskeminitis were known to the oldest inhabitants.

There is also a gas well at Crooked creek, near South Bend, Armstrong county, not indicated on the map.

No. 9. Tarentum, on the Allegheny river, above Pittsburg; the salt wells at this point, which descend to a depth of 450 feet, have always found more or less Petroleum within 350 feet of the surface. Some of these wells have been drilled exclusively for oil and have produced from eight to ten barrels per day. The oil separates by the subsidence of the brine and does not impart any flavor to it.

No. 10. Wells on Hosmer run, on lands of the Atlas oil company and others, near Garland, in Warren county; found an amount of oil at a depth of 500 feet, which would indicate the existence of a larger bed of sand-rock in the vicinity; for some reasons all operation has ceased for several years.

No. 11. Edinburg, Lawrence county, Pennsylvania, on the Mahoning river. A 10 barrel well 260 feet deep. No sand-rock is found until a depth of 100 feet is reached. In 1861, the Strawbridge well on the Mahoning river, produced 15 barrels a day for some time. Heavy oil.

No. 12.

No. 13. Gas well at Meadville, Crawford county, Pennsylvania. Six feet of sand found at 350 feet. No other sand, more than a few inches in thickness, had been found at 1,000 feet.

No. 14. Well on Stewart's Run, Venango county. Gas, of 150 lbs. pressure, struck at 150 feet in the second sand. Third sand not found at 825 feet.

No. 15. Coal on Cherry Run, one and a-half miles above Plumer, Venango county, on the Eagle farm, 75 feet above the bed of the creek.

No. 16. The Gas Wells of Erie, Pa., vary in depth from 450 to 1,200 feet. That of Mr. Deming, at the planing mill between Peach and State streets, found it at 453 feet. The average depth is generally about 600 feet. The depths at which gas is supposed to be found in a body, is often subject to a great deal of uncertainty and question. Anything so penetrating and of so light a density as gas from hydrocarbons will not, of course, be confined to fixed horizons; the gas of a very shallow well may rise through a natural crevice from a much lower point. Well of Fortuna Oil Company, French street, 585 feet, small amount of heavy oil 28°. Jareki and Company, 2 wells, one 1,200, one 700 feet deep. Brevillier's well, 625 feet, has been running five years. Conrad's brewery 600 feet. There are, in all, about 27 wells drilled for gas in Erie.

No. 17. Middlesex, Mercer county, Pa. A small well of heavy oil at the saw mill between Middlesex and Pulaski, on Erie and Pittsburg railroad.

No. 18. Well on Little Scrub Grass creek, Butler county, near Anderson's mills, at a depth of 1,000 feet found a third sand, and penetrated to the depth of 30 feet.

No. 19. Newell's Run, Washington county, Ohio. Well on the land of Robert Routand, below the mouth of the run, 5 barrels, 525 feet deep. Well on land of J. B. Kiggins, 10 barrels, 236 feet deep. These wells are on the main Ohio anticlinal belt before mentioned.

No. 20. Coal bed at Kinzua creek, near its mouth, twelve miles up the Allegheny river from Warren, Pa. The bed lies between 600 and 700 ("638") feet above the river, and is described as follows:—Cannel coal 4 feet; fire-clay below it 7 feet; bituminous coal below this 4 feet.

No. 21. Coal in Cherry Grove township, Warren county.

No. 22. Bradford, M'Kean county, Pa. The conglomerate here is found on the hill-tops, with some fine exposures, and a small amount of oil and gas is found in a few wells in the valley, whose record, if preserved, would be interesting.

No. 23. Heavy oil at Mecca, Trumbull county, Ohio.' Shallow wells and quantity limited.

No. 24. Bully Hill District, south of Franklin, Pa. The sand-rock here is 25 feet in thickness. Painter Well, Pope farm, 100 barrels, the other farms are the Ryle, Stroman, Wise, Miller, Graham and Holstein.

No. 25. Coal at Millerstown, found near the tops of the hills at an elevation of about 240 feet above the river.

No. 26. Well on Thorn creek, two miles west of Saxonburg, Butler county, claimed to have produced for a short time, a considerable quantity of oil.

No. 27. Well of Brown & Co., Jennings Ralston farm, Sugar creek, Venango county, above Cooperstown, 660 feet deep, 8 barrels of oil per day.

No. 28.

No. 29. Gas well at Corry, Pa., 950 feet deep.

No. 30.

No. 31.

No. 32. Heavy oil in a well at Wilcox, Elk county, Pa., at a depth of 1,691 feet.

No. 33. Conglomerate outcrop, North Rocks, near Warren, Pa., between Ackley and Hatch Run Glade township; conglomerate 40 to 50 feet thick, fine exposure, rests on slate, is covered with disintegrated sand-rock.

No. 34. Well at Olean, Allegheny county, New York; depth of well 785 feet; first sand at 300 feet; second sand at 450 feet; third sand at 780 feet; third sand-rock being very thin, some oil, much gas.

No. 35. Designates the situation of the heavy oil district of West Hickory; small wells, about 20 barrels found in an upper sand, and before referred to.

No. 36. Smith's Ferry, Ohio, is just over the State line, and some of the production is within the State of Pennsylvania; the oil produced is heavy oil, 27° to 33° gravity. The wells lie mostly on the road between Smith's Ferry, Ohio, and Ohioville, Pa., and the average production of each well, is from 25 to 90 barrels per week. The production of the entire district in February, 1869, was 250 barrels per day.

No. 37. Well on Winter's farm, Troy township, Crawford county, Pa, on Big Sugar creek, one and a half miles from the Diamond, ten miles west of Titusville. A good sand was found at 600 feet 56 feet thick, drilled to 1,670, but found no oil; torpedoed at 600, feet, small amount of oil obtained.

No. 38. Gas well, three miles north-east of East Sandy Oil district; a good sand-rock of 42 feet, much gas, no oil; one-half mile east of this, another similar well.

No. 39. Gas well, half way between Gas City and Lineville.

No. 40. Trace of oil in a well on Hiram Heath farm, Hickory township, Forest county.

No. 41. The *Newton Gas well*, on the A. H. Nelson farm, five miles north of Titusville, is 786 feet deep to a third sand, and immediately upon its completion, it began to discharge an immense volume of gas; the three-inch pipe from the well was divided into seven two-inch jets, one of which was sufficient to run the engine with an indicated pressure of 75 pounds to the square inch, the other six being left open; a measurement of the entire production gave the amount of four millions of cubic feet per day. Lines of pipe were laid from this well to Titusville, and have supplied light and fuel to a great number of dwellings and manufactories. The greatest objections to the use of natural gas, are its impurities and the pulsations of the pressure, rendering it difficult to regulate its use. It would seem, however, that the latter could be easily remedied.

No. 42. Octave district, Hyde farm and vicinity, near Titusville, sand-rock 50 feet; Abbott and O'Hare tract, wells 890 feet.

No. 43. The Drake Well, four and a half inches in diameter, the first in the oil region, was found in a surface sand at a depth of 71 feet; the well was subsequently drilled to the depth of 480 feet, but never afterwards produced much oil.

No. 44. Walbridge Farm, Sugar creek, Venango county; sand-rock, 25 feet. Smith Well, Ware farm, Lake branch of Sugar creek, five barrels per day of 42° oil, at 750 feet.

No. 45. Johnson Farm, Raymilton, Venango county; Raymond Well, 930 feet deep, eight barrels per day.

No. 46. Cowanshannock Well, on Portage creek, above Emporium, Cameron county, Pa.; no oil, great quantity of gas.

No. 47. The gas well at Fredonia, Chautauqua county, New York; the record of this well is given in the remarks upon the section on Map B.

No. 48. Gas wells of Neff and Ward at Niles, Ohio.

No. 49. Gas well of J. H. Casement, at Painesville, Ohio. Record as follows: Drift clay and gravel, 40 feet; Erie shales and soapstone, 648 feet; Huron shale, very black and bituminous, with strong smell of oil, 12 feet; total depth, 720 feet. Gas found in the Erie shales.

No. 50. Rock City, Allegheny county, New York; a fine exposure of conglomerate well known.

No. 51. Small show of oil on Blyson's Run, in Little Toby, Clarion county, Pa.

No. 52. Greene county, Pa.; Vance well on Little Whitely creek, Maple farm, near Dunkard creek; 150 feet deep.

No. 53. An exposure of conglomerate at Panama, New York, on both sides of Little Broken Straw creek; also known as "Rock City."

No. 54. Gas well at Howeville, Tionesta township, Forest county.

No. 55. White Oak, West Virginia. Oil from 26° to 28°; gravity found from 80 to 380 feet; Sand-hill is two and one-half miles north-west of White Oak; at a surface distance of 300 feet; the same gravity of oil is found in one well at 300 feet and another at 600 feet; in one well a lubricating oil of a yellow color is found at 300 feet.

No. 56. A salt spring at the head of Sugar creek, Crawford county, which has yielded a considerable quantity of salt. The water not being very strongly impregnated with saline matter, a well was sunk to the depth of 300 feet, but instead of yielding strong brine, oil was obtained in small quantities, and mixing with the salt water rendered it valueless.

No. 57. Groce Farm, Clarion county, between Clarion and Shippenville; small well 700 feet deep.

No. 58.

No. 59.

No. 60. Sage Run, near Oil City. Hill wells from 800 to 1,100 feet; sand-rock 60 feet thick.

No. 61. Wells on Dunkard's creek, Greene county, Pa.

No. 62. Well at Panama, Chautauqua county, New York, 550 feet deep; six feet in the second sand. A surface sand found at 344 feet, 75 feet thick. A first sand found at 461 feet, 30 feet thick.

No. 63. Jamison farm, Allegheny river, above Tionesta. Well 240 feet deep, sand 13 feet thick, small production of 48° oil. The well drilled 550 feet, but no more sand found.

No. 64.

No. 65. Five or six wells on Kinzua creek, Warren county, near the Allegheny river.

CHAPTER III.

GEOLOGY OF PETROLEUM.

The prominent facts concerning the relative situation of the horizon of the oil bearing sand-rock, illustrated by a section accompanying Map B, from Lake Erie to the Ohio river.

The knowledge of the strata underlying Western Pennsylvania may be obtained in two ways:

First. By observing the long and continuous outcrops exposed on the hill slopes above water level. These are seen to be not perfectly horizontal, but to sink steadily and slowly as we go southward and westward; (a formation which crops out in the State of New York, will be found at a great depth in Pennsylvania.)

Second. From the records of artesian borings, when duly connected with accurate levels of the surface.

The outcrops visible along the shore of Lake Erie will, of course, underlie any outcrops found south of that point, and the records of the wells drilled on the shore of the Lake, will furnish us with the character of the yet lower formation.

While the precise location of the horizon, at which our Pennsylvania oil is found, can only be determined by an examination of its entire area, a few deductions from such prominent facts as are not likely to be seriously affected by future work, will be of value in obtaining some idea of the nature of the search required.

It is particularly desirable to convey to the mind of the reader, an accurate impression of the relative size and location upon the surface, of such areas as outline the oil bearing rocks below, and these are defined on Map B. It will be observed that these spots are isolated and disconnected, and, with the exception of the stretch of the great lower oil fields, do not comprise any continuous belt.

To present this more clearly, it may be stated that out of 3,115 square miles of land in Pennsylvania, embracing everything which, by general acceptance, can be denominated as the oil region, only 39½ square miles have actually produced oil; that is to say, all the territory that now is, or has been producing,could be contained in an area of 25,000 acres.

Whether the component materials or the great body of this oil exist in the sand-rock where it is found, or at a depth beyond the present reach of the drill, is a question of scientific interest, but not of direct importance. What we are searching for to-day, is the location of the *vent holes* by which this oil reaches within drilling distance of the surface of the earth, whether such vent hole consists of an open sand-rock or sponge as in Pennsylvania, or of an anticlinal or system of broken rocks as in West Virginia.

From the fact, that coal and similar minerals are mined in continuous beds, stretching often over counties and States, it would be natural to suppose that the sand-rocks of the separate oil districts are connected in the same way.

The extent of the beds of the upper sand-rocks, near the surface of the earth, is so much greater than that of the oil bearing rock, that the proposition is substantially true so far as they are concerned, with the exception that they are not found at a positively uniform horizon, but overlap and underlie each other at the edges.

A well drilled anywhere in the region, will find a first sand, and sometimes a second and invariably some mountain sands, as they are called, are found even above these, but no productive sand-rock has been found on the horizon of the third or oil producing sand, except where indicated on the map.

Oil has been found in small quantities in the first and second sand-rocks, in detached spots, and from the earliest wells, but the bulk of the product has been obtained from the third sand. From the means within reach at present for defining the position of this rock, there is every reason to believe that it is situated approximately throughout the region under consideration on the same geological horizon.

A producing spot in the Pennsylvania region, (as defined on Map B,) is an area overlying, from 500 to 1,500 feet, a bed of porous conglomerate from three to seventy-five feet in thickness, the thickest part of the rock giving the best well, and this thickest part being generally found in the centre of the area, the rock tapering off at the edges.

When a well is drilled in an untried locality, and the third sand-rock found of any thickness, whether with much or little oil, this well is followed by others situated in different directions from it, until the thickest part of the sand-rock is discovered and a good well is the result and it is not long before the edge, where the rock *thins out*, can be mapped on the surface of the ground above it.

There is, therefore, within reach of the drill, no continuous bed of oil bearing sand-rock, but a series of scattered disc-shaped deposits whose outline and situation so far as discovered are indicated on Map B. These separate and detached beds of third sand-rock are lens-shaped, being thin at the edges as before stated.

The use of the term oil belt, has led to some misconception; lines which were run across the surface of the country for many miles in courses varying from north 14° east to north 22° east, have been found to intersect the surface directly over these producing beds of third sand, but in sep rate places and widely apart. The value of this discovery is doubtless confined to the extent of the conformity of these lines with the general course of the current which transported the material to form the deposit.

The Section on Map B.

For the purpose of locating the relative horizons of the oil-bearing sands, from our present knowledge, a profile section has been made extending through the length of the oil region from Lake Erie to the Ohio river.

In presenting this outline of the underlying strata of the oil country, it is essential that such a section can only state such general points as may be deduced broadly but still without question, in the present state of our knowledge from an extended view of the whole area involved.

Except so far as they present the main features, it is not desired that they should be considered final and conclusive.

In the profile given from the Ohio river to Lake Erie we have simply the line of the oil bearing sand-rock located at twenty-five different places, from a careful average of a number of wells at each place, and the height of each place above tidewater also, three horizons of the coal measures, with termini at well-known places.

The alignment begins at Marietta, on the Ohio river, following up the Ohio to Pittsburg, thence up the Allegheny to the mouth of Oil creek, up Oil creek to Titusville, and thence by levels of Dunkirk, Allegheny Valley and Pittsburg railroad, over the ridge to Dunkirk, on Lake Erie.

The points given in the section would seem to prove that all the oil sand-rocks of the region, even if they be disconnected and scattered through the strata at irregular distances, lie at about the same general geological horizon.

In the gas wells shown upon the section the position of the sands found has been omitted, not only to distinguish and separate them readily from the oil producing wells, but because the sands found in them so far as known were light and inconsiderable.

In the record of the Fredonia gas well, near Lake Erie, at the beginning of the section, we notice an entire absence of sand-rock. The outcrop of the lowest oil conglomerate mustbe sought for on the surface before reaching the shore of Lake Erie.

The record of the well is as follows:

50 Black shale, 50 feet.
80 Gray shales, 30 feet.
Black shale, with some gas and no water, } 120 feet.
200 Alternate black and gray shales, }
500 Soapstone, with occasional hard shales, 300 feet. Gas obtained here.
800 Black and gray shales, alternate, 300 feet.
1,050 Gray shale, 250 feet.
1,250 Limestone, 200 feet, and drill not through it.

The lowest sand-rock, therefore, as yet reported by any oil driller, is in the deep well of Mr. Jonathan Watson, which was drilled on the flat, in the City of Titusville, at a point 1,195 feet above sea-level, and in which a sand twenty feet thick and containing some green oil, was said to have been passed through at a depth of 1,976 feet. This sand was described as a white pebble conglomerate similar in every respect to the ordinary third sand.

The next highest sand-rock found, is the reported third sand of Watson's deep well, at a depth of 1,507 feet from the surface, which probably corresponds in horizon with that in the gas well at Corry, and the wells on the Tunaunguant creek, near Limestone village, N. Y. The well at Limestone being situated to the east, and that of Corry to the west of our alignment, would make the horizons at those places respectively higher and lower as the section shows.

In the absence of further detail at present, concerning the operations in the extreme northern part of the oil field, the few facts which could be relied upon, are chiefly valuable, as links to connect other more important data.

We come now to the lowest third sand of the oil region proper, which is found at Tidioute, at a depth of 140 feet below the first bench on the river, but not at a corresponding depth under the hills on either side. The sand-rock there if it be the same, it considerably higher, but when penetrated, in the hopes of finding the river sand, only "knocked the bottom out of the well."

No small amount of oil has been produced from a first sand at Tidioute, which is found on the river at a depth of less than 100 feet. On the river bank of the Economy tract, a well was struck in a crevice at 99½ feet in 1861, which produced oil steadily for a period of eight years. Four other producing wells in the vicinity were not over 150 feet in depth.

From Enterprise and Titusville to Oil City, the third sand, which is found in the two placed mentioned at an average depth of 450 feet, follows nearly the fall of the water-shed, being found at Oil City at a depth of 475 feet and along Oil Creek almost uniformly between these points.

At Petroleum Centre there appears to be a similar deviation, and also at Church Run, near Titusville, which a closer investigation may explain.

Surface oil has, likewise, been found in the first and second sand-rocks on Oil Creek. The Drake well, the first drilled for oil, found the sand at 71 feet, and produced, for some time, 25 barrels per day.

Some wells at Miller farm also found oil, for a short time, at 225 feet, in what was probably a split first sand. Both of these points are shown on the section.

The fall of the sand-rock progresses uniformly through intervening sections, until we reach Scrub Grass, on the Allegheny river. Here the alignment of our section, to preserve its accuracy, must be transferred bodily eastward, until we strike the line of the great lower oil belt.

We find here, that while the oil-bearing sands on Beaver creek are also apparently uniform in general horizon with the dip or fall we have had north of them, yet from this point southward along the belt the dip is much more rapid, so much so, that without the fortunate coincidence of the lowest line of water-shed with the direction of the development, the wells would, before this, have attained a very undesirable depth.

The explanation of the phenomenon of a fourth sand, as it is called, which is found on the cross belt from Armstrong Run to Greece City, and its precise geological location, would necessarily require the closest research. Whether it is a separate sand-rock deposited by a cross-current on a lower horizon, or whether it is only a divided third sand is yet a matter of question.

We find the formation immediately above it, almost identical with that above the third sand of the grand belt. A thin hard shell which caps it, is found in a similar position at Millerstown. The levels taken so far, seem to indicate that it occupies the same position as the third sand.

The fourth sand, at Karns City, is twenty-five feet thick, of a red and yellow color, and lies about seventy feet below that known as the third sand.

CHAPTER IV.

THE ECONOMICS OF PETROLEUM.

Section 1.—*Statistics of production, cost and proceeds of the product from the beginning to date—the net earnings of the entire region.*

During the fifteen years which have passed since the striking of the Drake well, the Pennsylvania Oil Region has produced up to January 1, 1875, sixty-seven millions seven hundred thousand barrels of oil, which brought at the wells, the sum of two hundred and thirty-five millions five hundred thousand dollars. Of this amount, 3,200,000 barrels are stored to-day in the tanks of the Oil Region.

The following table of production, price and export, will show more fully the progress of the business from year to year:

YEAR.	Production in barrels.	Average price for the year.	Amount.	Barrels ex-por'd crude, equivalent.	Crude, value of export at the wells.
1859....	3,200	31 cts. gal.	$41,664 00	....	....
1860....	650,000	16 "	4,368,000 00	....	....
1861....	2,113,600	$2 73 bbl.	5,770,128 00	27,812	$75,926 76
1862....	3,056,606	1 68 "	5,135,098 08	272,192	457,282 56
1863....	2,611,359	3 99 "	10,419,322 41	706,268	2,818,009 32
1864....	2,116,182	9 66 "	20,442,318 12	796,824	7,697,319 84
1865....	3,497,712	6 57 "	22,979,967 84	745,138	4,895,556 66
1866....	3,597,527	3 73 "	13,418,775 71	1,685,761	6,287,888 53
1867....	3,347,306	3 18 "	10,644,433 08	1,676,300	5,330,634 00
1868....	3,715,741	4 15 "	15,420,325 15	2,429,498	10,082,416 70
1869....	4,215,000	5 85 "	24,657,750 00	2,568,713	15,026,971 05
1870....	5,659,000	3 80 "	21,504,200 00	3,530,068	13,414,258 70
1871....	5,795,000	4 35 "	25,208,250 00	3,890,326	16,922,918 10
1872....	6,539,103	3 75 "	24,521,636 25	4,276,660	16,037,475 00
1873....	9,879,455	1 84 "	18,178,197 20	4,981,441	9,165,851 44
1874....	10,910,303	1 17 "	12,765,054 51	4,903,970	5,737,644 98
	67,707,094	3 48 bbl.	235,475,120 35	32,490,971	113,950,153 26

Total production, 67,707,094 barrels; average price, $3 48; total value of yield at wells, $235,475,120 35; total amount exported, 32,490,971 barrels; total value at wells of crude oil exported, $113,950,153 26.

The refining of this oil at a cost of two dollars per barrel, on seventy-five per cent. of the total amount, makes an additional value of over one hundred millions.

There has been exported a crude equivalent of thirty-two and a half millions of barrels, the value of which, at the wells, without refining, freight or handling, was one hundred and fourteen millions of dollars.

The freight on forty millions of barrels to the seaboard, at an average of $2 50 per barrel, would amount to one hundred millions. So that the value received from abroad for the export, would exceed at a minimum estimate, the sum of two hundred and sixty millions of dollars.

The total number of wells drilled in the region from the start to January 1, 1869, on or near actual producing territory, was 5,560; the amount of oil produced up to January 1, 1869, was something less than 25,700,000 barrels, giving the entire average production of each well at nearly 4,600 barrels. The amount realized for oil up to January 1, 1869, gave an average of $4 06 per barrel, or $18,700 for each well.

From that time forward until the present, the outline of the underlying strata being better understood and defined, and the failures proportionately less, the figures are as follows:

In 1869, there were drilled - - - -	991	wells.
In 1870, " " - - - - - -	1,007	"
In 1871, " " - - - - - -	946	"
In 1872, " " - - - - - -	1,032	"
In 1873, " " - - - - - -	530	"
In 1874, " " - - - - - -	433	"
*Total from 1869 to 1874, inclusive, - -	4,939	"

At round numbers, five thousand wells have been drilled since January 1, 1869, producing forty-two millions of barrels, at an average price of $2 91, giving a production to each well of 8,400 barrels, and a gross earning of $24,500. Of the 10,500 wells that have been drilled on or near actual producing territory, 3,250 are pumping to-day, with an average production of less than ten barrels each.

It will be seen that during the last six years, we have nearly doubled the average entire production of a well, with but a slight increase in gross revenue. It will also be observed, that three hundred wells drilled before January 1, 1871, are pumping to-day.

Making a fair allowance for wells recently started, we shall have the average life of a well at a little over two and one-half

*This estimate of wells drilled, is exclusive entirely of those bored on outside non-producing territory.

years. The annexed table and diagram are given to illustrate this point.

If the cost of drilling the 5,560 wells up to January 1, 1869, was $4,000 each, the cost of drilling was $22,240,000. If the cost of drilling the 5,000 wells since January 1, 1869, was $6,000 each, the cost of drilling was $30,000,000. Assuming 8,000 wells to have been a success, and to have averaged a life of two years each, at a cost of $10 per day for all expenses and shut downs, the cost of pumping would be $58,400,000.

The cost of 39½ square miles of actual producing territory, 25,280 acres at $500 per acre, $12,640,000. The Petroleum account, therefore, of the actual producing territory only, taking no account of failures or outside operations, is as follows:

Total amount received at wells, to Jan. 1, 1875,		$235,475,120
Cost of drilling, - - - - -	$52,240,000	
Cost of pumping, - - - - -	58,400,000	
Cost of territory, - - - - -	12,640,000	
	123,280,000	
Profit, - - - - - -	112,195,120	
	235,475,120	235,475,120

The net profit, therefore, of producing 67,700,000 barrels of oil, was $112,200,000, or $1 67 cents per barrel. If it were possible to include in any statement of this kind, the amount expended in "wild catting" and speculation, it is doubtful if the net profit would amount to $1 per barrel.

Much more information of interest can be deduced from the tables given, but it is better that the estimates should be made by the parties who seek it. One further instance only will be given.

We received in 1874 for our oil at the wells,	$12,765,000	
We paid for drilling 433 wells @ $5,000, -		$2,160,000
We paid for pumping 3,300 wells, $5 ℔ day,		5,940,000
We have increased our stock of crude on hand, 1,400,000 barrels, @ $1 17, -		2,380,000
Balance, - - - - - - -		2,285,000
	12,765,000	12,765,000

Section 2.—The method of drilling and pumping wells. Illustrated by Plate A.

Before our time, the art of drilling artesian wells had attained a degree of perfection which was considered remarkable; the tools of the famous well at Grenelle in France, which were thought worthy of minute description in the standard works of reference at the time, are to-day little else than objects of curiosity.

The driller of the Drake well, with a set of tools which he could almost carry on his shoulder, slowly making his way through the first seventy feet of sand-rock, and the driller of to-day making no account of fifteen hundred feet and a six inch hole, with drilling tools weighing over two tons, will serve to indicate comparatively the advance that has been made in the art of artesian boring. It suggests the thought that where so much has been accomplished, the maximum limit of depth to be economically attained cannot yet be said to have been reached. One or two things in reference to this are worthy of notice.

The Pennsylvania regions are so far advanced in this art, that all former and even present operations of this nature, in other parts of the world, dwindle into comparative insignificance; the perfection thus far attained has, doubtless, been reached by the enterprise and intelligence of men from all parts of the country, but exercised and brought to completeness within the limits of the region itself.

So much so, that of the vast number of appliances successively introduced, the outside world has supplied to the region but little else than the raw material; of late years, approved patterns of engines and boilers have been made elsewhere, but the immediate contrivances for the work must be forged and wrought under the eye of the operator himself. Probably such a community, consisting almost entirely of young men, has never been gathered together within reach of the great business centres. The facility with which patents were obtained, and the protection given by the law, has aided materially in the rapid strides made in the work.

It would hardly be desirable within the limits of this report, to describe more than the main features of the method as it

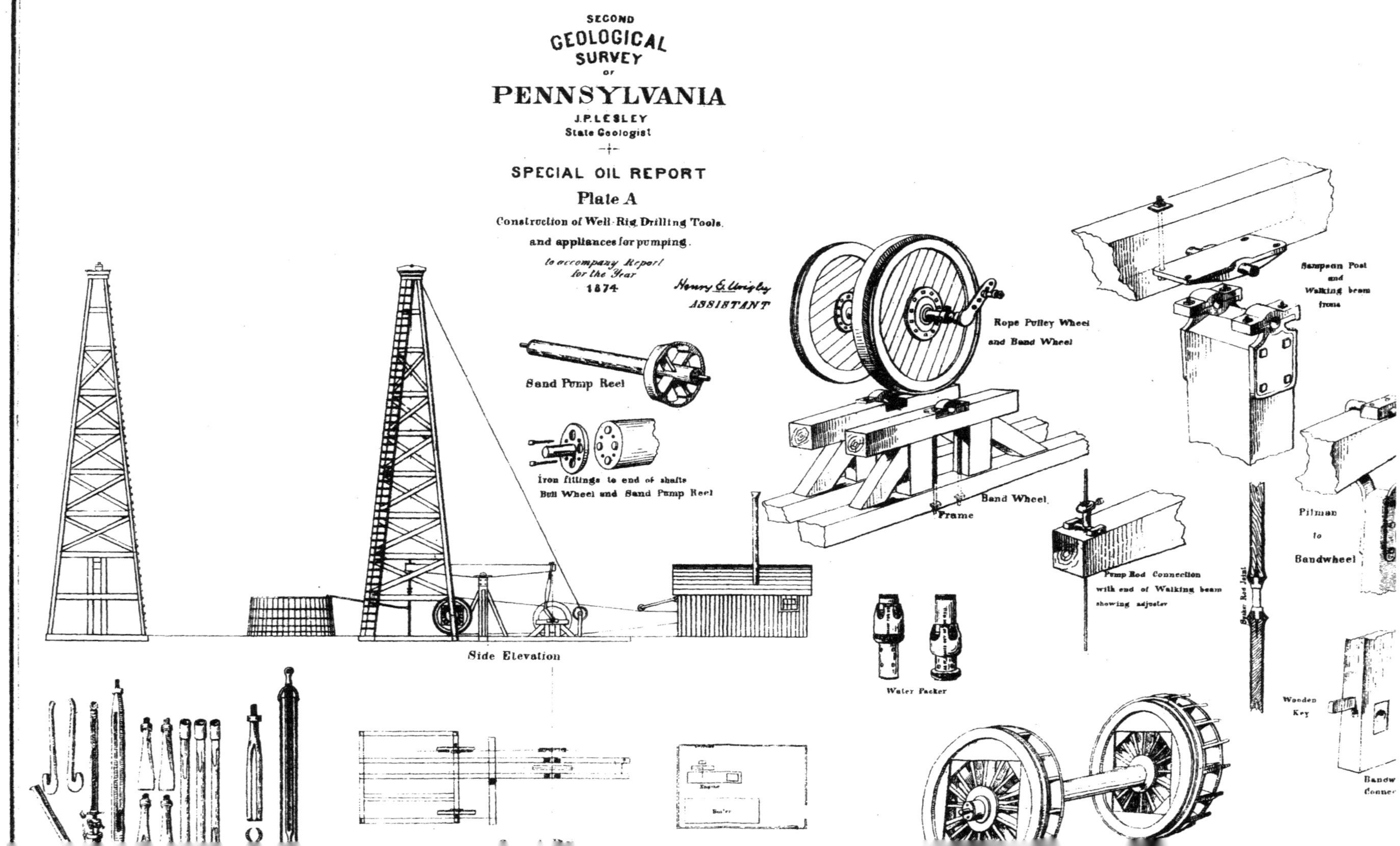
SECOND
GEOLOGICAL
SURVEY
OF
PENNSYLVANIA
J.P. LESLEY
State Geologist
SPECIAL OIL REPORT
Plate A
Construction of Well-Rig, Drilling Tools,
and appliances for pumping.
to accompany Report
for the Year
1874
Henry E. Wrigley
ASSISTANT
Sand Pump Reel
Iron fittings to end of shafts
Bull Wheel and Sand Pump Reel
Rope Pulley Wheel
and Band Wheel
Band Wheel
Frame
Sampson Post
and
Walking beam
frame
Pitman
to
Bandwheel
Pump Rod Connection
with end of Walking beam
showing adjuster
Sucker Rod Joint
Water Packer
Side Elevation
Engine
Boiler
Wooden
Key

exists to-day, still less to include even the most valuable inventions relating indirectly to well boring.

The Rig.

The Rig is composed of a derrick, band-wheel, bull-wheel, sand pump reel, sampson post, walking beam and engine house. The present derrick is built "balloon frame," 16 to 20 feet square at the base, and from 60 to 72 feet in height, resting on hewed oak sills 12 by 18 inches, framed and pinned at corners; the four corner posts are of pine plank 10 by 2 inches, spiked together at right angles, and connected with cross-ties and diagonal braces of 8 by 1½ inches; the top holds the usual cast iron derrick pulley, and a ladder to reach it is constructed upon one side.

The bull-wheel now in use is shown in the plate; four main arms of oak 8 by 2½ inches, pass clear through the shaft and are locked and keyed; the false arms between, 6 by 2 inches, wedge upon each at the shaft and are firmly held by the three thicknesses of pine boards forming the outer rim.

The total length of oak shaft is from 10½ to 12 feet, and its diameter 13 inches; its length between wheels 6 to 7 feet; diameter of wheels 6½ to 7 feet, and bearing pin on ends 2½ by 4 inches; the manner of securing the iron bearing pin and plate to the end of the oak shaft, as shown in the plate, does not appear at first glance to be as substantial as the severe test of practice has found it.

The brake is a simple iron strap applied under the bull-wheel as shown, and a wooden pawl is used to fall from above, against the arms, as a permanent stop when desired.

The band-wheel is built of inch pine lumber, surfaced to a uniform thickness, the present diameter being about 7 feet; the rope pulley wheel on one side is 5 feet, and the face of the wheel 9 inches. The grooves of the rope pulleys on both band and bull-wheels are made of hard wood, and to insure a perfect outer circle, the edges are turned off after the wheels are firmly mounted on the shaft and revolved on temporary bearings.

The sand pump reel has always been the most awkward part of a well rig; acting as a friction pulley against the band-wheel with the bevelled face necessitated by the different angle of the shaft, its tendency was to self-destruction, even when most carefully and securely fitted up. A solid wheel of hard wood with wooden keys, is sometimes used, also a piece of casing as shaft, with a cast iron pulley keyed upon it.

The reel shown in the plate is an oak shaft, about 8 feet in length, 8 inches in diameter, with arms of the wheel passing through the shaft and enclosed with an iron rim.

The sampson post and walking beam have gradually increased in size, until the one is a post 20 inches square and the other from 24 to 26 feet in length, with a section at the centre of 30 by 18 inches. The great weight of the walking beam, has perhaps some of the effect of a fly-wheel, where a fly-wheel nevertheless is not found to be a practical success.

The utmost care is shown in making the foundation of the sampson post and band-wheel frame perfectly solid and substantial; two long hewed sills for the latter, not less than 12 by 20 inches in section, pass clear under the derrick sills; the jack-posts, cap and braces of the band-wheel frame as shown, being of pine 10 by 12 inches, the cap bolted through to the sill.

The Well.

To Col. Drake we are indebted for the invention of the driving pipe, which, if patented at the time, would have been the foundation of a handsome fortune; as a means of passing through soft overlying earth to the rock, it probably never will be excelled. The pipe used, at present, is eight inches in diameter, of cast iron one inch thick, driven down into the earth in sections of eight feet in length, connected with wrought iron bands, heated and shrunk on.

Putting down a thin iron pipe of six inches diameter below the lowest fresh water vein, and retaining the surface water by a water packer between the outside of the pipe and the wall of the well, enables the driller to proceed in his work without any annoyance from this source; and when the well is completed, to take his tubing in or out of the well at pleasure, still keeping the water permanently from the oil bearing rock. In fact, the entire operation of drilling and pumping is carried on through the casing, and not until a well is finally abandoned is the casing drawn.

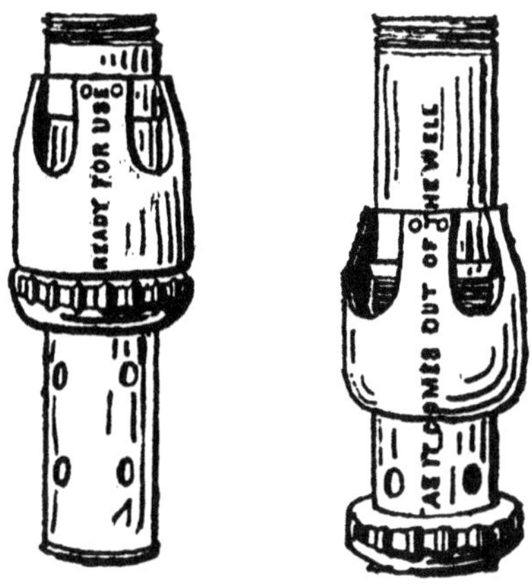

Water Packer

In this connection the water packer shown, (see *plate*,) is a wonderful improvement on the bag of flaxseed formerly used; the weight of the column of water presses the leather against the sides of the well, forming an effectual stopper. By means of a left handed thread it can be loosened in a few minutes, and drawn out of the well without difficulty.

Motive Power.

The main and most desirable features of a drilling engine, are simplicity of construction, durable alignment, and an adjustable cut-off permitting close economy in the use of steam.

While it takes the full power of an engine to drill and draw tools expeditiously, it requires but a small fraction of that power to pump, so that when one boiler is furnishing steam to three or four wells, it is essential that each engine should take the minimum amount required.

This is accomplished in the link motion of the eccentric, where, by adjusting the link, the steam will follow the piston from one-fourth to five-sixths of the stroke, leaving the balance of the stroke to be worked by expansion.

The engines now in common use are from 12 to 15 horse power, the boilers from 15 to 20, to give ample steam for drilling, and to pump a number of completed wells, the steam pipes to the several engines being boxed with non-conductors, to prevent condensation.

Drilling Tools.

A set of tools, to-day, weighs from 1,800 to 2,600 pounds, and costs about $350. They consist of a temper screw, rope socket, auger stem, sinker bar and substitute, the jars, two bitts, a round reamer, a flat reamer and two wrenches.—(See *plate.*)

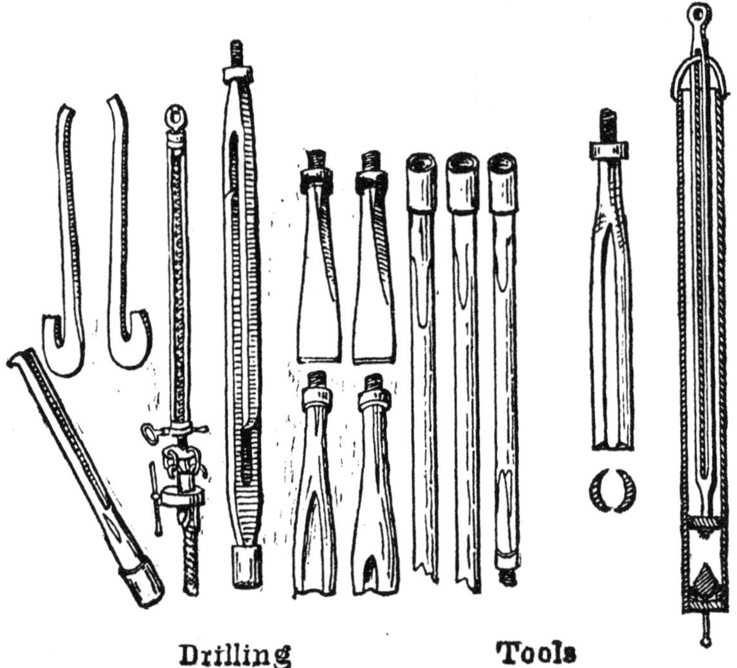

Drilling Tools

The temper screw varies little from that in former use, except in size, the present length being about 5 feet. The auger stem, sinker-bar and substitute are, respectively, 24, 14 and 5 feet in length, the latter being used in starting a well.

They are made in the body, of common round iron, (2½ to 3 inches,) with boxes and pins of Norway iron. Pins are 2¾ inches in length, 2⅜ inches in diameter, 8 threads to the inch, and with the least possible taper, to prevent being loosened by the constant jar, which also has a tendency to crystalize the iron in the pins and boxes, making it necessary to renew them at intervals.

The Jars are made entirely of Norway iron two inches square, with the exception of the inner faces and ends of the slotted openings, which are lined with steel; the whole being heated red-hot and carefully annealed, to effect a thorough union of the metals. The stroke of the jars has been reduced to 12 inches, and their total length is about 6 feet.

The Bitts are made of Norway iron, with 40 pounds of steel on the point, which is drawn to a width of 5½ inches, more or less, according to the size of the well.

The flat and round Reamers are made also of Norway iron, with more steel on the point; there are also various extra tools for different purposes.

The hollow Reamer for straightening a crooked hole, is shown on the plate. A spud or spoon for enlarging the well around a stuck tool, is simply half a hollow reamer; a slip socket, to drop over the head of a tool that is fast, with dogs or teeth to fall out and catch under the collar; a horn socket, or tapering iron tube, to drive and wedge upon the head of any fastened iron. All these, with many others often especially devised and constructed for the purpose, are required at various times in sinking a well.

The cable used is 6 inch untarred manilla rope; the wire rope has not yet been made that will answer for drilling purposes, as none are sufficiently pliable to use on the shaft of a bull-wheel, and to increase the diameter of the shaft would cause loss of power.

The sand pump has two improvements: first, the valve with a drop stem to open it on reaching the bottom of the well, and second, the piston which keeps its place at the bottom of the pump while being lowered, but when drawn up, fills the pump by its suction with the loose debris and water.

Pumping.

The main improvements under this head may be included in the two items of sucker-rods and valves. The old style of sucker rods with fish-tail ends, has long since passed out of use; the rivets constantly becoming loose and dropping into the working barrel were a great annoyance. To remedy this we have a joint without any rivets, where the wood is driven into a metal socket and widened at the end with a wedge, (as shown in the *plate*,) an intermediate piece of small tubing, making a screw connection between the two sockets.

The valves in use are a plain standing valve at the bottom of the working barrel, and a three or four cup valve or a water packer of some kind; especial valves are made for gas when it predominates largely in a well, and to meet the several conditions which occur. The body of the sucker-rod is made of the best upland ash, 1½ inches in diameter, and in length from 24 to 28 feet.

As an instance of the energy with which this business has been prosecuted, it may be stated that over 3,800 patents bearing upon the production and manufacture of Petroleum have been issued since the striking of the first well.

Section 3.—*Pipe Line Transportation. Pipe lines, their construction and capabilities, comparative value of this method of transportation.*

The first producing wells being found upon the flat land of Oil creek and the Allegheny river, the removal of the product was not a matter of great difficulty; flat-boats loaded with oil in barrels and sometimes in bulk, conveyed the oil down stream to the nearest railroad. The railroads gradually extended their branches along the valleys of the region in all directions, but the oil produced from inlying valleys or remote spots, had to be conveyed in barrels by team from the wells to the dump tank at the shipping station, often a distance of ten or twelve miles, and at a cost of as much as three dollars per barrel.

To remedy this, it was natural to turn to the conveyance of water in pipes as an example, and in consequence a four inch cast iron pipe with leaded joints, was laid in 1861 from Titusville, four miles down the creek.

Owing undoubtedly to its imperfect construction, it leaked so badly under the slight pressure to which it was subjected and was such an alarming failure, that all projects of the kind were abandoned until the year 1865, when Mr. Samuel Vansyckle conceived the very happy thought of extending the tubing of the well as it were, to the station desired, however distant, and laid the first line of two inch tubing six miles in length, from Pit-hole to Miller farm, having two intermediate pump stations which were subsequently abandoned as unnecessary.

The mechanical success of this line soon caused the matter to be taken up by others, and the length and capacity of the lines extended over the upper, and finally over the lower region, until at present the net work of pipes which, like the veins of a human body, extends throughout the entire country, reaches with the branches to the wells, the enormous aggregate of nearly two thousand miles.

Without intending to specifically describe the extent and capacity of the several lines, it is desirable to direct attention to the peculiar and unexpected advantages of this mode of transportation, and to note the discovery of some valuable facts concerning its economy and the possible range of its usefulness.

There are to-day, in the oil region, fifteen separate companies engaged in the transportation of oil by pipe from the wells to the railroad.

The Octave Pipe Company gathers up the oil from the wells of Church run and Octave districts, and loads at Titusville.

The Church Run Pipe Company is confined to the wells at Church run, delivering at Titusville.

The New York Pipe Company has a main line from Tidioute and West Hickory through the New London, Colorado and Enterprise districts, 13 miles, without relay; also a line from West Hickory to Garland, on the Philadelphia and Erie railroad, 15 miles, with a relay pump station half-way.

The Titusville Pipe Company has a line from Pit-hole through the Shamburg and Pleasantville districts to Titusville, eleven miles.

The Pennsylvania Transportation Company has a net work of lines of about 150 miles in length, draining the Pit-hole, Pleasantville, Shamburg, West Hickory and Octave districts, shipping at Titusville, Miller Farm and Oil City. The line from

West Hickory to Titusville pumps thirteen miles without a relay. The company also operate a ten mile line and connection in the lower region, from Millerstown to Brady's Bend.

The Rochester and Oleopolis Pipe Company has the only successful gravity pipe line ever put in operation; it is six inches in diameter, and formerly delivered the oil from the Pit-hole district to the railroad at the mouth of Pit-hole creek.

It has also a line laid from Oleopolis over the hill to Oil City, which is an ordinary 2 inch line.

The United Pipe Lines reach almost every part of the lower oil region, and aggregate over 500 miles in continuous length. Their main lines are from Turkey run, at the head of the great lower oil belt, to Oil City; from Modoc and Fairview to Raymilton, on the Jamestown and Franklin railroad, over 22 miles; from Karns City, Millerstown and Greece City to Harrisville, on the Shenango railroad, three lines, twelve, fifteen and sixteen miles each.

The Union Pipe Company is side by side in length with the United Pipe, draining the entire lower region by innumerable short lines to the Allegheny Valley and Pittsburg railroad, and shipping to Butler and Coyle's station, on the West Pennsylvania railroad, by main lines of fifteen miles in length; the total continuous length of main lines, and connections, being more than 500 miles.

The American Transfer Company, from Upper Turkey Run to Emlenton, has about 50 miles of main line and connections.

The Antwerp Pipe, and the *Oil City Pipe*, extends from the Petersburg district to the Allegheny Valley railroad, and to Oil City through the Sandy district.

The Grant Pipe Company, from the Grant farm above Parker's landing, delivers on the river, and is 30 miles in continuous length.

The Relief Pipe Company, from Story farm and Armstrong run, also delivers at the river, and is one of the most prominent routes of transportation for the oil in the lower region.

The Columbia Conduit Company is the forerunner of a formidable competition of the pipe line, as a means of transportation, compared with a railroad, and its main line of three inch pipe extends from Millerstown, Butler county, to the mouth of Deer creek, above Pittsburg, on the Allegheny, a distance of 37 miles, having two relay stations on the route; the connections, from the receiving tanks to the wells, will probably add forty miles more. All these pipe lines are shown, in detail, on the published maps of the region.

General Construction.

The tubing in common use for well and shipping purposes, is made of wrought iron plates, of number 6 or 7 wire guage, heated in a furnace and closed around a cold iron core; the joint in the lap-weld tubing being formed by passing it, while hot and soft, through a series of rollers, which first turn up the edges, and then press or weld them down upon each other.

In butt-weld tubing, the edges are simply heated to a white heat, and then rolled together.

Tubing, to be merchantable for oil purposes, must stand a test of 1,200 lbs. per square inch of internal pressure, a strength which is attained only by lap-weld.

In a pump for a pipe line, the essential elements are a long stroke, a small oil cylinder, and a large steam cylinder.

The air chamber also of the pump must be proportioned to the work of the line, for the capacity of the pump is substantially the capacity of the line. There should be no obstruction in the line, especially at the point of delivery; a simple bend of the pipe at the receiving tank will add many pounds of pressure to the pump.

All the stop-cocks and connections should be free way stopcocks. If the passage through the plug of a cock is but two-thirds of the sectional area of the pipe, for all the purpose of a pipe line, the diameter might as well have been just that much reduced.

The experience acquired in the construction and management of pipe lines in the oil region, has shown the comparative economic value of this method of transportation to exceed all others yet devised. Whether this fact is applicable in any way to our advantage, in the face of existing arrangements, or the uncertain life of oil production, may be left for subsequent examination.

The point itself seems to be so valuable to the public at large, that it is only proposed here to give such items of detail as will enable any one to satisfy himself of the truth of the proposition, and leave the consideration of its application to any future need that may arise.

The use of this method of carrying is based, of course, upon the quantity of the fluid, to be carried, being ample and correspondingly cheap. To arrive at an estimate of the relative values of railroad and pipe line transportation at the present time it is necessary first to state, that the computation of the working capacity and required force of a pipe line is taken entirely out of the old channels of the conveyance of water by heads, by the overwhelming predominance of the element of friction. From 75 to 80 per cent. of the pumping force required by a pipe line is necessary to overcome the friction dependant on the velocity of flow.

Also, that in building a line, if the pipe were made very heavy, one pump would force it a long distance and save the cost of labor and fuel attendant on intermediate stations; but, that if there were a great many intermediate stations, the pipe could be made very light and the expense of construction greatly reduced, while the cost of fuel and labor is greatly increased.

It is evident that there is a mean length of line which can be operated to advantage by one pump. With the lines at present in use this is about fifteen miles; with care in the construction of the line it could be extended, without doubt, to twenty miles.

Let A B fig. 1, represent a pipe line; A being the pump station where a pressure say of 900 lbs. per square inch is required, and B the point of delivery at the tank fifteen miles distant, where there is no pressure at all; it is evident that in the construction of ordinary lines, which are of equal thickness for their entire length, there is just twice the amount of iron used that is actually required.

In removing this unemployed iron from our line, let us make our section as follows: See fig. 2; the gain accruing from an expansion of the bore of the pipe will be shown by the following figures, which are given to represent the construction, cost, and working capacity of a twenty mile pipe, of an average diameter of three inches.

Fig. 1.

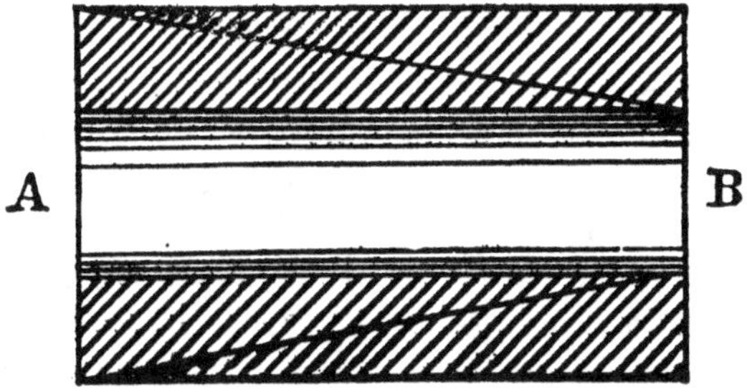

Fig. 2.

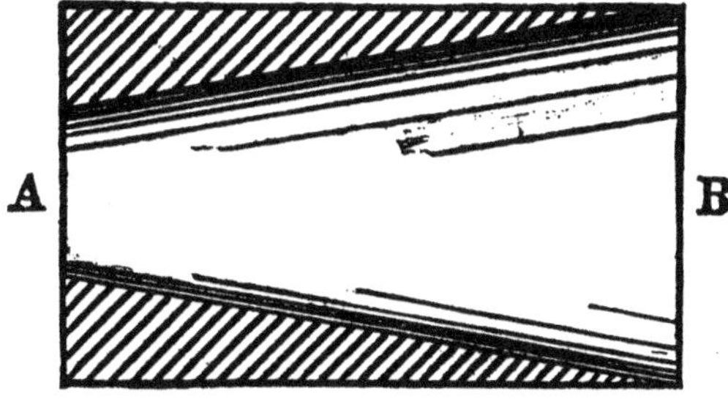

The area of internal section of a three inch pipe is 7.06858344 square inches; contents of line (20 miles) 105,600 feet, 38,776 gallons or 901 barrels; to deliver 3,600 barrels per day would require a velocity of flow of five feet per second.

Weisbach's formula to ascertain the head required to overcome friction, is as follows:

$$(.0144+\frac{01746}{\sqrt{v}})\times\frac{l}{d}\times\frac{v^2}{5.4}=h'$$

h' = head required in feet.
v = velocity in feet per second.

l = length of the line in feet.
d = diameter of the pipe in inches.

This formula applied would be,

$$(.0144+\frac{.01746}{\sqrt{5}})\times\frac{105600}{3}\times\frac{25}{5.4}=2473.9$$

In practice this is found to be, for these long pipes, about 25 per cent. in excess, where the route is carefully selected and the line properly laid. As these lines follow vertically the contour of the ground in a hilly country, this is somewhat remarkable, especially when it is considered that no account is taken of any increased friction for the rise of the line in many places above the hydraulic mean gradient, from the highest point to be overcome to the point of delivery.

If the line be enlarged every five miles, we shall have as follows:

5 miles of	3	inch pipe friction head required	618.5
5 "	$3\frac{1}{4}$	" " "	570.9
5 "	$3\frac{1}{2}$	" " "	530.0
5 "	4	" " "	464.0
Total,			2,183.4

Being a saving in head of nearly 300 feet.

It will be readily seen that an equivalent to this gain may be obtained by a reduction of the diameter of the pipe at the pump, or by an increased velocity, thus:

		Velocity.	Friction head.	Contents of section.
5 miles	$2\frac{3}{4}$ inch,	5 ft. 9 in. per sec.	674.9	187 bbls.
5 "	3 "	5 ft. per sec.	618.5	225.2 "
5 "	$3\frac{1}{4}$ "	4 ft. 2 in.	570.9	264.5 "
5 "	$3\frac{1}{2}$ "	3 ft. 6 in.	530.0	306.8 "
			2,394.3	983.5 "

Being still less than the friction head required for a continuous three inch pipe.

It will also be found that the reduced line contains 983.5 barrels instead of 901; and since the element of friction represents the greatest resistance to be overcome, the enlargement will simply cause a constant reduction of velocity, and therefore of friction and pressure.

In twenty miles of straight pipe there will, probably, be elevations to overcome. Let us assume 400 feet as an extreme, and add it to the head required, we should then find the total head as follows:

	Head required.	Pressure in lbs. to sq. inch.
At the pump, 2¾ inch pipe - -	2,794.3	1,212
Beginning of second 5 miles, 3 inch pipe,	2,119.3	919
Beginning of third 5 miles, 3¼ inch pipe,	1,500.9	651
Beginning of fourth 5 miles, 3½ inch pipe,	930.0	403

(It will be observed that the head of 400 feet is carried through all the sections in the absence of given levels of any actual line; otherwise the heads and pressures, for the last two or three sections, would be very much reduced.)

The formula of Weisbach, from which the above has been calculated, was based upon the results obtained from water; by multiplying the pressures given by the difference in specific gravity of water and the oil of commerce, .7972—we have the following

	Pres. in lbs. per sq. inch.	Thickness of metal in pipe.	Weight of pipe per foot.
1st section, - -	969	.167 inch	6.709 lbs.
2d " - - - -	735	.138 "	5.537 "
3d " - - - -	521	.093 "	3.799 "
4th " - - - -	322	.071 "	2.910 "

Our first section will contain - - -	177,117 lbs of iron.
Our second " " - - -	146,176 " "
Our third " " - - -	100,320 " "
Our fourth " " - - -	76,824 " "
Total, - - - - - -	500,437 " "

The weight of the line if made of the ordinary two inch tubing in the usual manner, would be 387,235 lbs.; and its capacity for delivery would be but 1,000 barrels per day, against 3,600 in the line above described.

The work of the line would equal 366,291,200 gallons raised one foot high in twenty-four hours, requiring for its exertion a horse power of 77 for water, and 62 for oil.

From the above data we make the following estimate of the cost of the twenty mile pipe:

500,437 lbs. iron @ 9 cents, delivered on ground,	$45,039 33
10,000 lbs. fittings @ 20 cents, - - - - -	2,000 00
Laying pipe in trench 2 ft. deep, 6,400 rods @ 60 cents,	3,840 00
70 horse power boiler, pump and station, complete,	10,000 00
Telegraph line, - - - - - - - -	2,000 00
1,000 barrel tank, iron, - - - - - -	1,000 00
Sundries, - - - - - - - - -	1,120 66
	$65,000 00

To move this 3,600 barrels of oil per day, would require the direct services of four men; two engineers relieve each other at the pump every twelve hours, one man receives the oil from the wells and keeps the guages, and one man receives and ships the oil at the railway station.

The cost of an engine and train of thirty-six tank cars, which would be required to carry 3,600 barrels of oil, would exceed the cost of the entire pipe line, exclusive of any estimate of the cost of the roadway, which is about ten times the cost per mile,

With an ample supply of the fluid, and the required number of these twenty mile sections, the estimate made would cover any distance required.

No further object is aimed at in these statements, than to instigate a full investigation of the possible economic value of this method of moving fluids. The figures given will be found within safe practical limits, and based upon actual experience.

Section 4.—Refining. Composition and properties of Oil; the regulation of its manufacture to secure safety; fire-test and sale of Oil by weight.

The preparation of Petroleum for use in the lamp, is of course a business of no greater age than the article itself; it is true, that the process followed to some extent that of the destructive distillation of bituminous shales; but beyond the suggestion of the main outlines of the method pursued, there is no similarity in the practice.

There has existed, until recently, a vast deal of misapprehension in the general mind, of the nature, properties and "failings" so to speak, of Petroleum Oil; the dangers attending its use have been both underrated and overrated, and the exact point of danger is necessarily difficult to locate.

Among the majority of people who use refined petroleum, and even among those to whom the question of fire-test is a matter of interest, the impression prevails that it is a simple fluid, like water, which, by sufficient heat, is resolved into a single gas or vapor.

A thorough comprehension of this point is essential to a foundation for any further consideration of the safety and properties of the article. All Petroleum consists of an unknown number of distinct hydro-carbons, which the writer believes will include the paraffine series, the olefine series, and a few members of the aromatic series.*

Investigation has not yet been sufficiently minute to determine the precise number of members in each series, or to disprove the possibility of the existence of intermediate series.

On the basis above stated we find that crude petroleum consists of not less than thirty distinct and known hydrocarbons, which are separated from each other merely by different degrees of heat, many others unknown undoubtedly exist, to which no special individuality has as yet been given.

The refined oil of commerce has been freed from both the lighter and the heavier members of each series, and, for the purpose of illustrating its relation to crude oil, is assumed by the writer to consist of the paraffins ranging between $C^6 H^{14}$ and $C^{13} H^{28}$, the olefines ranging between $C^6 H^{12}$ and $C^{11} H^{22}$, and the last two or three members of the aromatic series.

Such, however, is the peculiar nature of the lightest vapors,

* Fowne's Chemistry, American edition, 1871, p. 507

that they never can be absolutely expelled, but seem to blend and cling as it were to the heavier paraffins.

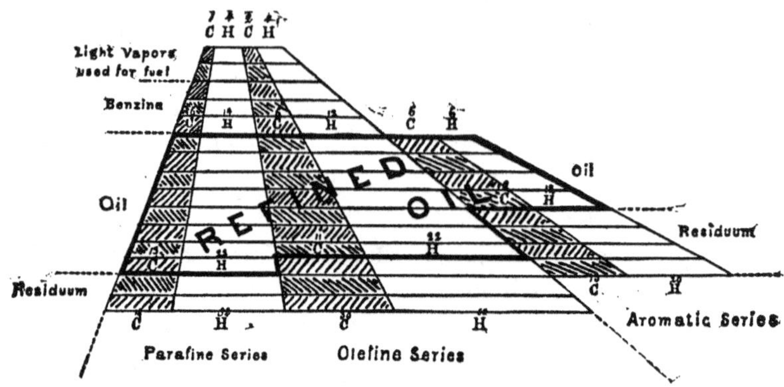

Fig. 3.

Diagram of Crude and Refined Oil.

The relation of the component parts of refined and crude oil will be more readily understood by the accompanying diagram. A perfect distillation of refined oil, consists in removing the separate members of this structure in their regular order as shown, just as a building is taken down brick after brick, or without "cracking," (to use the technical term,) or decomposing any one member of the several series; the heat being applied very gently at first, and steadily increased, just enough heat being applied to the oil to remove the member remaining uppermost at the time.

The crude oil, say of 46° gravity, is first subjected to the mild heat of steam pipes, which throws off the lightest compounds in the form of gas, which is used for fuel. After being subjected to this treatment, the oil is placed in the still, free from any compound of higher gravity than 75°. The body of the still, and the brick casing, retaining, (as is especially the case in large stills) some of the heat of the last run, this prevents any decrease in the temperature of the oil.

The fires of the still being carefully graduated to a steadily increasing heat, there are thrown off through the vapor pipes of the still the following products:

First. A product of 80° to 70° density, known as light naphtha or gasoline.

Second. Benzine, from 70° to 65° density.

Third. Heavy benzine, from 65° to 62°; this benzine being put back with the crude oil and run again.

Fourth. Burning oil, from 62° to 43°; the stills being run off at 43°, that is to say when the residue in the still acquires that density; this residue can be treated in special smaller stills, and be reduced in great part to burning oil. The success of this stage of the process is dependent entirely upon the adjustment of the heat applied to the constantly changing composition of the oil; it cannot be attained by simply keeping a low temperature, and taking ample time; for while experience has shown that crude oil may, if desired, be reduced almost entirely by a slow heat to benzine and tar, there is no method known of reversing the process and making oil from benzine.

On the other hand, any greater heat than is absolutely necessary to remove the several members of the series, successively, will destroy the color of the oil by setting free some of the carbon.

Between this "Scylla and Charybdis" lies the highroad to success in this manufacture.

The percentage of refined from crude, got by careful averages from large runs estimated semi-annually, is from 70 to 72 per cent. It is claimed by some that this percentage can be greatly increased, but it is considered desirable to state here, only such facts as are known to exist at present.

The vapor on leaving the still is dashed with a spray of cold water, which not only condenses at once some of the heavier members, but washes out and separates any loose carbon or soot that may come over in the vapor. The remaining vapor, uncondensed, is passed through a worm of iron pipe submerged under running water, of such length that no vapor will come out with the "distillate," as it is called, which runs out of the tail pipes. This distillate is treated as follows:

First. With sulphuric acid, to remove the tar and bleach the oil.

Second. Washed with clean water to remove the acid.

Third. With caustic soda, to neutralize the acid, and

Fourth. With ammonia, to complete the neutralization.

Fifth. Washed again with water.

The agitation of the oil being effected, during all these processes, by air-pumps. The oil is then exposed to the sun, in open tanks, under glass, for twenty-four hours, or more if it be desired, to bleach it further, and improve it generally.

The Measurement and Sale of Refined Oil.

The inevitable and annoying differences arising from the variance in the guagings of refined oil in barrels, and the possibility of making barrels which would defy an accurate guage, led to the adoption, by the leading exporters and refiners, of the sale of oil by weight. The barrel is weighed and marked, then filled with oil and weighed again, the difference being the amount of oil contained.

The basis on which oil is sold is as follows:—Oil of 110° fire-test, 45° gravity, will weigh 6½ lbs. to the gallon. Oil of 125° fire-test will weigh about 2 pounds more per barrel than oil of 110° fire-test.

Sixty-five barrels of 110° fire-test oil, 45° gravity, weigh, without packages, 19,536 pounds.

Sixty-five barrels of 75° benzine weigh, without packages, 16,270 pounds.

The advantages of this system have become so apparent, that no further remark is necessary than to call attention to it.

Fire-test.

The detection of dangerous oils, and the protection of the public at large from the danger attending their use, is a matter which has not yet been fully accomplished. The difficulties encountered are as follows:

First. Benzine, and the lighter members of Petroleum, make the brightest and most beautiful light, and can be burned in any lamp with perfect safety, so long as they are kept at a temperature sufficiently low to keep them from vaporizing, which of course is ordinarily impracticable.

Second. While the weight of refined oil increases uniformly with its gravity, the fire-test does not, but is irregular.

Third. The facility with which refined oil from the larger refineries, (almost invariably safe and of good quality,) can be adulterated with the lightest gasoline, at any stage of its progress to the consumer.

Fourth. The imperfection of the present fire-test.

Fifth. It is the nature of all oil to settle and arrange itself in any vessel in stratiform layers, so that the heavier oil will be found at the bottom and the lighter oil on top; this can readily be tested in any vessel, large or small, which has stood some time. In an oil that is not *uniform*, the difference between the top and the bottom fire-test of a barrel is often as much as five or even ten degrees; so that the sample for fire-test should be taken from the top of the vessel instead of the bottom, as at present.

Against these points we might offset the following suggestions:

First. To a certain extent the best oil weighs the most. While the difference is not great, and the statement is not sweepingly true, yet a standard minimum weight for a gallon of oil would exclude a great part of the dangerous oils. If we find an oil of high fire-test and light gravity, it indicates that it is only a mechanical combination of the extremes of the series—very heavy with very light members of the series of hydrocarbon compounds—and it is apt to separate and arrange itself as stated before, if left long standing.

Second. For the reason just stated, the gravity of the oil, should within certain limits, correspond with the fire-test; a light oil in the ordinary acceptation of the term, will burn up quickly in the lamp—a heavy oil last much longer.

Third. All the explosive oils here considered being hydrocarbons, the excluding of the presence of any of the lighter hydrocarbons from a certain point, in any composition whatever intended for illuminating purposes, would cover most of the ground. While this would totally extinguish many patent burning fluids which are placed in the market whenever Petroleum commands advanced prices, there would be no injustice done.

Fourth. When the consumer knew that the lack of a certain weight in an ordinary gallon-can indicated danger, and that it would burn up quickly, he would, in connection with the color of the oil, have a simple and ready means of judging for himself; skillful adulteration might dissolve some substance that would add to its weight and gravity, but to accomplish such adulteration without detection through the ordinary tests of color, odor and burning properties, to say nothing of tests, means would be almost impossible.

It should, however be well understood that safety and a high fire-test means a poor burning oil and a dull light; it is a question simply between safety to the consumer and the brilliancy of the light, each being attained at the cost of the other.

An oil of 110° fire-test contains, without question, all the elements of safety, and possesses an amount of brilliancy which far surpasses anything of a higher fire-test.

In burning a lamp, as in refining, the lighter parts of the oil will pass off first; hence, an oil of 150° fire-test may burn brightly at the start, but will finally become dim, on account of the greater density of the balance.

A standard fire-test of 110° of samples from the top of a package that had stood twenty-four hours undisturbed, a standard minimum weight per gallon sufficient to exclude all oils outrageously dangerous, and finally the outlawing of all hydrocarbons lighter than a stated formula in any composition intended for burning, would embody the elements of both safety and comfort to all who use Petroleum or shale oils.

Refining Capacity.

The refining capacity of the United States, may be stated as follows:

In the Oil Region, - - - - -	9,231	barrels per day.
New York, - - - - - -	9,790	" "
Cleveland, - - - -	11,732	" "
Pittsburg, - - - - - -	6,090	" "
Philadelphia, - - - - - -	2,061	" "
Baltimore, - - - - - -	1,098	" "
Erie, Pa., - - - - - -	1,168	" "
Boston, - - - - - -	3,875	" "
Buffalo, N. Y., - - - - -	631	" "
Portland, Me., - - - - -	350	" "
Other small refineries, - - -	200	" "
Total - - - - - -	46,226	" "

Section 5.—The uses of Petroleum, crude, as a preservative. Refined oil as an illuminator; residuum, naphtha, hydrocarbons, as fuel.

Crude oil is, probably not excelled as a preservative for timber, and makes a principal part of almost all compounds which have lately been proposed for that purpose; as a single ingredient, it seems to lack penetrating properties; but timber which has been thoroughly saturated, by lying a long time in crude oil, seems to have become almost imperishable.

The acids contained in all crude oil show their greatest effect in the pipe-lines through which it is in constant motion. This singular result is observed, that only certain sections of the pipe seem to be attacked, in some cases being eaten almost through, while other parts are left unimpaired.

The crudes, from different sections of the region, vary somewhat in gravity, but are valued for refining purposes chiefly in proportion as they are free from clay and earthy impurities.

Church Run, near Titusville, yields the best crude, of about 46° gravity, yielding a greater percentage of refined than any other. Pleasantville and West Hickory a black oil of 47°, and the lower region a light green oil of 47°. The oil at Pit-hole was the lightest ever found. the gravity reaching, in some cases, as high as 51°.

Heavy oil, from 28° to 35°, has always a greater amount of earthy matter, and an amount of sulphur which renders it undesirable for refining.

The difference between black and green oil seems to depend only on an additional amount of clay, or other mineral substances in the former.

The illuminating power of refined oil decreases almost directly with its gravity and increase of fire-test. Benzine and the lighter products are so brilliant, that the temptation to use them in some form is constantly presented. Oil of 150° fire-test is, in comparison, positively dull when the lighter parts are burned off.

The safety of all oil is increased by age. Left standing undisturbed, the lighter parts pass gradually off, but the oil will then burn with a dull light.

The amount of crude oil produced from the bituminous shales being in this country only from 40 to 140 gallons per ton, the crude shale oil cannot be placed on the market at much less than $2 per barrel, notwithstanding the fact that distillation gives a number of minor products which are used in the arts.

The standard fire-test required by Great Britain is greater than that of Germany or America; and yet the earlier use of the shale oils there has introduced a great number of burning fluids, which are really much more dangerous than any Petroleum.

Our refined Petroleum has penetrated to the most distant parts of the world, it brightens the long winter nights of Sweden and Norway, and even Iceland, it is sent to Australia and New Zealand, to China and Japan, to Russia, Germany, Austria, France and Great Britain, in the face of the fact that in every one of the countries named, surface oil or bituminous shales, exist in quantities that would seem to be fatal to competition.

The predominance which our oil has obtained, is due solely to the fact that it contains a greater proportion of the lighter products than any surface oil found elsewhere. Nature has distilled it for us from the shales, and we take directly from the well an equivalent to the first product of the coal oil still, but containing also a much greater proportion of those members which possess illuminating properties.

Whether the drill in other countries as with us, would find a light oil on the edges of the present foreign oil territories or even within their limits, is a question that some day may interest us.

Russia is following up closely an investigation of her oil fields on the Caspian sea, and has employed American workmen; in Peru, Americans have been granted large concessions of territory, and have produced a considerable amount of oil.

Austria has made a thorough survey of her oil region in Gallacia, "dry holes" have been found in Sweden and Norway and a complete set of drilling apparatus, with experienced workmen, were sent from the Pennsylvania Oil Region to New Zealand.

Another valuable product from Petroleum is the residuum of the still, which is used for roof-tar, for preserving wooden pavements and for bridge timbers. Almost all of this product of the still in refining is used at present, to a greater extent than is generally supposed in the composition of lubricating oils. From nitro-benzine we have also aniline, which is chemically a powerful base, and a colorless oily fluid of a specific gravity of 1,020; it yields various beautiful colors, mauve or aniline purple, majenta or aniline red, (appearing commercially in the form of crystals of rosaniline, and which have an extraordinary power of coloring in proportion to their bulk;) aniline yellow or chrysaniline, aniline blue, violet and green. [There is a popular notion that the iridescent colors which are observed floating on the surface of coal oil, petroleum, and spring water issuing from coal mines and iron ore beds, are evidences of the presence of aniline and other colors in the substance of the material; but such iridescence is due to the action of light on thin films of any substance whatever.] *

Owing to the small quantities of material used in this branch of manufacture, it does not possess any special interest for us in this connection.

Benzine, so familiar from its use in a great number of the minor arts, next to burning oil, is the most valuable product from the crude.

Petroleum as Fuel.

The use of Petroleum and its kindred hydrocarbons, for the purpose of fuel, claims finally our attention and deserves some especial notice.

It is essential to state broadly at the outset, that the superiority of coal in calorific power over all other fuels, has never yet been disproved The appearance of a hydrocarbon fire indicates such intense heat, that the many earnest minds who were interested in its use, arrived very slowly at an admission of the actual results. The facts seem to be, that an average Petroleum has from one and a half to two and a half times the heating power of an equal weight of anthracite coal, their relative composition being—

Coal, hydrogen, 5; carbon, 83; ashes, 12; specific gravity, 1.42.

Petroleum, hydrogen, 85; carbon, 15; slight residuum; specific gravity, .825.

* Dr. Genth informs me that when he was personally interested in the manufacture of the aniline and other hydrocarbon colors, all efforts to obtain them from the American Petroleums proved abortive, and therefore he does not believe that the series of hydrocarbons of which they are characteristic exist in our rock oils. J. P. L.

Against this we have the almost equal offset, that a ton of Petroleum will occupy the space of $1.\frac{152}{100}$ tons of coal, and to this must be added the overwhelming difficulty, that crude oil at $2 per barrel, the lowest price it has ever reached on the seaboard, is four times the price of the same weight of coal.

The most practical commentary that has been made in the matter lies in the statement that with oil at fifty cents a barrel, the manufactories in the Oil Region burn coal, which commands there probably the highest prices known in the State.

Nevertheless, it is claimed with apparent sound reason, that the advantage in using liquid fuels lies not so much in any inherent superior heating power which they have in themselves, as it does in their clean and easy use, contrasting strongly with the waste of heat and the labor attendant upon the use of coal.

The strong draft, required for burning coal, necessarily carries much of the heat out of the chimney into the open air, and no attempt to remedy this has been to any great extent successful. Owing to the predominance of the volatile members of the liquid fuels, it has been proposed to so construct a fire-chamber, that the heat may be subtracted from the current of gas, from the fire, before it passes into the flue; and this, together with the labor saved in stoking, would show a valuable difference in favor of hydrocarbons. While the law is imperative, that so much heat is required for the decomposition of water as is evolved in the combustion of its constituents, yet we know practically beyond question, that the use of dry steam in jets adds vastly to the perfect combustion of liquid fuels.

Many complicated devices have been presented for this purpose; but it is not generally known that it can be accomplished with the greatest perfection by an extremely simple and inexpensive apparatus. A narrow pan in two parts, between which the jets of dry steam are introduced, a dome like cover with an opening in the top for the escape of the flame, and the whole so set in the fire-box, that all the draft shall come through it, will effect a perfect combustion without any escaping carbon or smoke.

Benzine has been used in this way, with entire success and safety, in many dwellings and small shops in the Oil Region. It is not found to be much cheaper than coal, but it does not involve the care of ashes or the trouble of starting a fire.

The pipe lines procure their fuel for their pumps by taking the gas and lighter products of the oil from their tanks, passing the oil through retorts heated gently, and returning it to the tank again improved in quality and value, the vapor being drawn off at the top of the retort and conducted to the fire-box.

CHAPTER V.

SUMMARY OBSERVATIONS.

It may be worth while, before closing this report, to draw a few general conclusions from the information which is here set in order.

A line drawn from the south-west corner of the State of Pennsylvania, at an angle of 45 degrees with its western boundary, or about north-east and south-west in bearing, will include broadly in the triangle which it forms with the west and north line of the State, all that part of our Commonwealth in which we may expect to find the great staple which has proved such a source of wealth.

Irrespective of any efforts that have been made beyond our boundaries and to the eastward of this line, the upper part of this triangle, dividing equally the west line and embracing three-fourths of its area, has been tested in every direction by nearly fifteen thousand wells.

Just how thorough and final this test has been, of course, the future will show. North of Oil City however, the examination has been so searching, that while some new isolated areas of sand-rock may probably be outlined, if the price of oil shall warrant it, there is still little or no prospect of a recurrence of the great production of earlier years.

With a view to meeting the questions: Whether we are over-estimating the durability of our oil fields? and what can be done to realize the greatest return and avoid waste? the following points seem to be worthy of remembrance:

Our everyday idea of the mining of all minerals is based, to a great extent, upon the older discoveries of coal and gold.

The special difference between the mining of coal, and other solid minerals, and of this fluid, lies mainly in the fact, that the former is not necessarily wasteful, the bed can be measured and estimated; and we know that we can go and get it when we want it, and stop when we please. We know also that operations on the land of one owner may be carried directly to his boundary line without affecting the interests of his neighbor.

But the oil sand-rocks which stretch under adjoining farms, are not only affected but often absolutely controlled by a few thoughtless operators, who own or lease territory adjoining that in which a good well has been found.

Developing a bed of rock is but a race between the owners of the surface above it, as to who shall first exhaust the basin of oil below the surface, common to all parties.

All this is highly disastrous; and the result has been, that whereas we know that a sand-rock, if kept free from the surface water and pierced by only a moderate number of holes will last eight or ten years, the average life of a well has not practically reached three years. We do not exhaust our beds of sand-rock, but destroy them. We pluck the apple, so to speak, by rooting up the tree.

It is this feature of oil production, which will decide for us, within the next ten years, whether we shall still lead in this commodity or remain only an example for some wiser Commonwealth to profit by.

Had it been possible from the start to regulate drilling, it can hardly be questioned that one-third of the wells that have been drilled, would have brought as great a return as we have had from them all thus far, and at one-third of the cost of producing.

The questions then naturally arise, what is the condition of our oil fields to-day? What are the prospects for the future, and can anything be devised to ensure the full production of oil territory and a greater return for labor and capital?

The answer to the first, and the basis of a fair estimate for the second part of this question, will probably be found in the new survey of this section when completed; the third is a problem not lightly solved.

Within the lines which have been defined on Map B, between the existing oil wells and gas wells, (for the purpose of giving shape and locality to the oil producing region,) we find the sand-rock producing heavy oil, lying in a range confined entirely to its north-western edge and so described. We find also, that the horizon of this heavy oil geologically is higher than that of the light oil sand-rock, and that the wells therefore are not so deep.

We find also a general fall or dip of the sand-rocks towards the south and east throughout the entire region.*

We find that the outline of these producing beds of sand-rock when traced on the surface of the earth, seem to bear in their sweep and general direction, the impress of the currents by and from which they were deposited, and from this may perhaps be obtained some notion of the possible location of other beds.

In view of the improved machinery for obtaining the oil from these beds, there is as yet no evidence that the increasing depth of wells going south will retard extension of the development, if the increase in depth of wells be gradual.

The consumption of oil has reached a point at which it becomes our interest to supply, not in wasteful abundance ruinous to the territory, and at a loss to ourselves, but with such restrictions as will not only give better pecuniary results, but enable us to secure the fullest return from every bed of which it is capable, and spreading the producting over a greater period of time.

Independent of the minor advances in the matter of detail which will probably be made in the refining process, there exists only room at present for such an increase of the percentage of refined from crude, as will equalize the price of benzine with that of burning oil; as the use of the former has attained to considerable proportions, this situation might occur by a decrease in the production, and without any other cause.

We find that the discovery of Petroleum in quantity was so ordered as to be practically co-incident with the beginning of the great war which called forth all our resources, that it paid during several years to the National Government, a direct tax of over ten millions of dollars, and that as an article of export it has brought a return from abroad of at least three hundred millions.

It will not be hard to discern that this great result is due less to any local advantages of fortune than to the untrammelled freedom which our institutions give to American enterprise.

---

* This of course holds good only down to the line of the Brady's Bend synclynal. Descending the Allegheny river from the Brady's Bend wells, the rocks are seen *rising* towards the south-east. Three miles below the mouth of Red Bank, they become flat and then descend south-eastward all the way to Pittsburg. In southern Butler and Lawrence counties, and in Washington county, the general dip is south. J. P. L.

II.

On a Map and Profile of a Line of Levels through the Butler, Armstrong and Clarion County Oil Fields; with a Geological Section from Well Drillings, by D. Jones Lucas, Resident Engineer.

The accompanying map and profile, by Mr. Lucas, mainly explains itself. It gives the location and height above tide (per Pittsburg datum) of fifty-four (54) well known oil borings, and the location of eleven (11) others, making sixty-five in all, selected from several thousand oil wells, put down along the principal belt of recent oil production, ranging about S. 45° W. through Clarion county, crossing the Allegheny river at the mouth of Clarion, and stretching away S. 22° W. through Armstrong and Butler counties, towards the Ohio river.

The total length of the section is thirty-six (36) miles.

Edenburg, Martina, Turkey City, Petersburg, Foxburg, Parker's City, Martinsburg, Petrolia, Karn's City and Millerstown are the names of places best known along the line, proceeding southward.

From Foxburg to Parker's City the line follows the Allegheny river, west bank. It then ascends Bear creek and passes over to the head of Buffalo creek and to the high land north of Butler.

Here the oil excitement of 1873–4 reached its southernmost limit. The profile shows how the oil-bearing sand-rocks bury themselves slowly deeper and deeper beneath the surface; the depth of well requisite to reach them increasing in proportion to the southerly dip of the underground, *plus* a southerly rise of the surface towards Butler; thus:

	Mouth of well above tide	Bottom of well above or below tide.	Depth of well.
Karne well at Parker, - -	884+tide.	29+tide.	855
R. S. Harrington well, Bear cr.,	1,150+	50—	1,200
Lightfoot well, Bear creek, -	1,190+	99—	1,289
Crage Farm No. 4, on the divide,	1,315+	199—	1,514

	Mouth of well above tide.	Bottom of well above or below tide.	Depth of well.
Hillside w. on Buffalo, (200 bar,)	1,291+	234—	1,525
Diviner w., " (900 ")	1,280+	250—	1,530
Asa Say w., descending creek, -	1,157+	370—	1,527
O'Conner, - - - - - -	1,146+	427—	1,573

But the further southward movement of exploration was arrested not because the wells became too deep, but because the "third sand," (in which all the above wells stopped,) lost its gravel, and therefore would not yield plentifully to the pump. This cause was reinforced by a ruinously low market price of oil, occasioned by the sudden doubling of the total daily American production, brought about in its turn by the rapid exploitation of the Butler county end of the line. Mere depth of well will never practically prevent, nor ever greatly check exploration, other things being equal. The Dry Hole well, for instance, was sunk from a hill-top overlooking Buffalo creek, at an elevation of 1,358 feet above tide, to a depth of 1,631 feet, *i. e.* 273 below tide. C. D. Angell's well, No. 9, a thousand feet distant from the Dry Hole, commenced on the same hill top, at 1,420 feet above tide, and must have been about 1,680 feet deep.

Eight wells in the profile descend to what is called the Butler county Fourth Sand. This adds a hundred feet to their depth, as appears by comparing the Lightfoot (third sand) and Nesbit (fourth sand) wells, lying close together at Petrolia:

	Mouth.	Bottom.	Depth.
Lightfoot, - - - -	1,190+	99—	1,289
Nesbit, - - - - -	1,196+	195—	1,391
Difference, - - -	6	96	102

Two of the fourth sand wells at Millerstown are selected by Mr. Lucas from the rest. The descent, southward, appears by comparison with the two above:

M'Desmit, - - -	1,195+	290—	1,485
Borough, - - -	*1,173+	312—	1,485

Descent in 6½ miles from Lightfoot to M'Desmitt, 191 feet.

This gives a rate of descent, in the fourth sand, of 191′ in 6.5 miles=30′ per mile.

*Possibly an error for 1,193, in which case the two wells will be almost precisely alike.

The rate of descent southward, in the third sand, between the Edward Bennett well (Bear creek) and the O'Connor well, (end of profile,) appears to be—

Surface,	1,025+	3—	1,028	depth,
	1,147+	426—	1,573	

a fall of 423′ in $18\frac{1}{3}$ miles; or 23′ per mile, S. 10° W.

This rate is not far different from that of the S. W. dip of the sand rocks in Venango county, as measured by Mr. Carll.—See his report, with underground contour-line maps of the upper and lower surfaces of the first and third sands; showing the shape of the Oil Creek synclinal.

The rate of descent along the Clarion end of the line, between the Ballat & Lee well and the Isabella well, on the Allegheny river, appears to be—

Surface,	1,355+	337+	1,018	depth,
	928+	140+	788	

a fall of 197′ in 13.8 miles=14′ per mile, S. 45° W.

This direction of S. 45° W., is almost parallel to the direction of the great bituminous coal basins and their separating anticlinals, the nearest anticlinal being that which arches the conglomerate in the river cliffs between Red Bank and Mahoning. We may, therefore, take this rate of 14′ per mile S. 45° W. as very nearly representing the fall of the whole country (underground,) synclinals and anticlinals together, towards the Ohio river.

To prove this, it is only necessary to take the rate between the Isabella, and Brown No. 1, along the river bank—

Surface,	928+	140+	788	depth,
	897+	3—	900	

a fall of 147′ in 3.5 miles; or 42′ per mile S. 3° E.

Could we get equally good elements of calculation for a rate of descent more at right angles to S. 45° W., we would doubtless find it to exceed 42 feet in the mile. For the rate increases as we box the compass in that direction; thus:

(*a*.) S. 45° W., rate 14′ per mile, (observed.)
(*b*.) S. 10° W., rate 23′ per mile, (observed.)
(*c*.) S. 3° E., rate 42′ per mile, (observed.)
(*a*,*c*.) S. 28° E., rate $45\frac{1}{2}$′ per mile, (calculated.)

No near approach to accuracy, however, can be made through these elements of calculation, because they are obtained along an extensive line of observation, and are subject to all the local variations of dip, or rate of descent. Combining (*b*) and (*c*), for example, would give the impossible result of a dip of 90′ per mile S. 65° E.=1°.

At the mouth, or along the lower end of Bear creek, there seems to be, on Mr. Lucas' profile, a large local perturbation of the regularity of the southward descent of levels. The upper profile shows it in a striking manner, because its vertical scale, originally exaggerated to *twenty* times the horizontal, is still left exaggerated *five* times as published. But the same perturbation appears quite as apparently in the *unexaggerated* profile which has been placed underneath.

This perturbation may be partly due to some error of record in the Parson No. 6 well; but of this there is no other evidence.

The perturbation is intensified by the fact that the profile line *descends the dip* from Brown No. 1 well to Parson No. 6 well, and then *re-ascends the dip* from Parson No. 6 to Donelly No. 6, and the Edward Bennett wells, thus:

<table>
<tr><td>Brown No. 1,</td><td>897+</td><td>3—</td><td>900′ deep.</td><td rowspan="2">S. 18° W.</td><td rowspan="4">S. 54° W.</td></tr>
<tr><td>Parson No. 6,</td><td>1,025+</td><td>130—</td><td>1,155′ "</td></tr>
<tr><td>Donelly No. 6,</td><td>972+</td><td></td><td></td><td rowspan="2">S. 66° W.</td></tr>
<tr><td>Ed. Bennet,</td><td>1,025+</td><td>3—</td><td>1,028′ "</td></tr>
</table>

A true strike, or dead level, is here seen along a line S. 54° W., between the Brown and the Bennett, for a distance of three and a half miles. The true dip should therefore be at right angles to this, S. 36° E. The map shows that the Parson No. 6 lies off this strike (or dead level) line joining the Brown and Bennett, 3,000 feet, down the dip (S. 36° E.) The difference in the level of the third sand is 130—3=127 feet. But 127′ in 3,000′ gives a rate of 223′ per mile, or nearly 2½°.

We have here, then, a comparatively steep plunge into the Brady's Bend synclinal. Whether this extra steep dip be locally confined to the mouth of Bear creek; or whether it be represented by a steepening of the dip to be noticed in the profile further south, approaching Petrolia; or whether we are deceived by some error in the record of the Parson No. 6, are questions demanding attention.

What renders this eccentricity of the "third sand" in the Parson No. 6 the more remarkable and the more suspicious, is the fact, plainly visible in Mr. Lucas' profile, that *no such change of dip occurs in the first and second sands above it.* It looks as if the well sinkers of the Parson No. 6 had missed the third sand and gone down to a stray fourth. Great confusion has arisen from such mistakes all over the oil regions. In fact, well-sinkers usually fix their attention too exclusively on the gravel-layers; and the coarse sand-beds are so frequently replaced by softer and finer sand-beds and by shales, that it is no wonder if some elements of uncertainty enter into the composition of all our geological sections of the oil regions. We are obliged, therefore, to confide in the accumulated testimony of several thousand wells, and in the local knowledge of the number, thickness and position of their "sands," acquired by intelligent oil men.

Perhaps the chief value of a profile section like this of Mr. Lucas is, that no one can look at it carefully without feeling a strong conviction that it expresses the real structure of the undergound, to a depth of one or two thousand feet beneath the present surface; although not a single well record, of all the sixty-five out of which it has been constructed, can be said to be perfectly and entirely reliable. In trigonometrical surveys, the observer can rely with perfect confidence on the *mean* of his hourly observations (if extended through an entire month) to a fraction of a second of arc. In astronomy, the *mean* of many thousands of observations of the times of the emersion and immersion of Jupiter's moons, is accepted as nearly perfect. So, in our profile-section a comparison of its sixty-five well-records, each imperfect in itself, proves beyond the possibility of serious error the following important propositions:

I.—That there are seven principal sand formations, viz:

(*a*) The sand rocks which outcrop on the hill sides of the highland of Clarion county, east of the Allegheny river, and of the highland of Butler county, west of that river. And these "surface" sand rocks include No. XII, or "the conglomerate" and "Millstone Grit" of our geological books:

(*b*) The "bluff sand" rock which forms the Allegheny river cliffs above and below Parker City. Hitherto considered to be the genuine No. XII conglomerate, this rock now seems to represent either the first and second mountain sands, or the second mountain sand alone, of Venango and Warren counties; the far northern outcrop of which is at the "Rock Cities" near Olean, and west of Chatauque Lake, in the State of New York:

(*c*) The (third) mountain sand, as in Venango county.

(*d*) A first oil sand:

(*e*) A second oil sand:

(*f*) A third oil sand, to which nearly all the wells of this profile section were put down; and

(*g*) A fourth oil sand, a hundred feet still lower, struck by eight of the wells of the section, at Petrolia, Karne City and Millerstown; three of these yielding respectively 900, 700 and 100 barrels a day.

Much must yet be done to settle definitely and exactly the equivalency of the various members of the Mountain Sand Series, some of which are probably double. But there can be no doubt about the wide out-spread and general regularity of these; nor that of the four oil sands beneath them. It must always be remembered that oil sinkers care nothing about the regularity and extent of sand rocks, except so far as they continue to be coarse and gravelly enough to hold an abundance of oil, and to give it out freely. Their attention is absorbed by the gravel patches, streaks, or belts, *in* the sand rock formations. For their purposes *where the gravel ends the sand rock ends.* Not so for the geologist. He must study the outspread of the sands, their number, order, thickness and distance asunder, whatever be their constitution; and where they are *not* gravelly, as carefully as where they are; where they are merely saturated with an oil which cannot be sucked out by the strongest pumps, as carefully as where they hold oil which will flow and spout the moment a vent to the surface is granted to it.

The whole theory of the origin and extent of the petroleum deposit depends upon a thorough study of the sands, no matter whether they constitute, in whole or in part, good oil rock or not.

II.—Irregularities of thickness of each sand are evident throughout this section, and throughout all such sections. All oil men are well acquainted with these irregularities. Their true cause is not yet understood; nor is it yet made very plain how they are connected with alternations of coarseness and fineness in the composition of the rock.

But certainly one instructive lesson has been learned, namely, that there is no apparent relationship between irregularities of thickness (and coarseness) of one sand, and irregularities of thickness and coarseness of another sand above it or below it. No relationship is visible between the irregularities of the oil sand and those of the mountain sands. They grow thick and thin, coarse and fine, each one for itself, and without regard to one another.

This must be especially true when the bottom oil sand and the top mountain sand, 1,000 feet vertically apart, are considered. Hence it appears entirely unreasonable to judge of the condition of the third oil sand, as some have professed to do, by observing the coarseness or fineness of the surface sand rocks. The two things have evidently no connection.

III.—Intermediate sand-rocks undoubtedly exist in many localities. These do not appear in Mr. Lucas' profile, nor usually in other similar sections, and chiefly for the reason that oil sinkers neither care for them nor wish to notice them, most wells being sunk on contract "to reach the third sand," and contractors being satisfied in their own minds, from their own experience or that of their neighbors, at about what depth they are likely, and indeed almost, if not quite certain, to strike the three principal sands.

IV.—In Clarion and Armstrong (according to Mr. Lucas' profile) the three oil sands are crowded close together, and the three mountain sands also; while a great interval (300–400 feet) separates the two groups. But in the new Butler region the oil sands lie as far asunder from one another as the first oil sand lies from the third mountain sand. This change in the character of the whole section is best seen in the lowermost representation of the profile section on the plate, because this is drawn to a true scale. The intervals between the sand-rocks are of course occupied by shale formations, in which mud predominates over sand, and no gravel beds occur and no oil is expected to flow.

Some of the above propositions will be made more clearly

manifest in Article No. 3 of this report, by means of a carefully measured section made some years ago along Slippery Rock creek, 25 miles west of the southern end of Mr. Lucas' line. But the demonstration of some of the most important points will be given in Mr. Carll's reports of the progress of the survey in the Venango county oil field.

The three oil rocks of Mr. Lucas' profile section pass far beneath such wells as are shown in the Slippery Rock section; in which, moreover, the mountain sands appear to carry oil. This is again true in the Little Beaver and Ohio river (Smith's Ferry) oil fields. In Greene county the oil bearing rocks lie many hundred feet above even the mountain sand series, viz: in the Barren Measures, between the lower or Allegheny Coal Series and the upper or Monongahela Coal Series.

On the other hand the new Beattie Well at Warren struck, at the end of March, 1875, light oil, flowing at the rate of several barrels per day, in a Sand lying at least 600 feet below the Third Sand of Venango.

The petroleum of Pennsylvania, therefore, must not be looked upon as confined to the three (or four) oil sands shown in Mr. Lucas' profile section. It ranges, in various districts, through at least three thousand feet of measures, and is of different qualities at different horizons. This is a strong argument against the supposition that it ascended by distillation from the deep, and was caught and held by the gravelly portions of the sandstone formations.

Another strong argument in the same sense is deducible from the fact that a few hundred feet of shale has, in most cases, effectually prevented the oil from ascending from the oil sands to collect in the mountain sands, or escape at the surface. It follows, as a matter of course, that one or two thousand feet of similar shale formations *underlying* the oil sands—(See Mr. Wrigley's profile section)—would be equally potent for preventing the ascent of oil from greater depths to collect in the oil sands.

A third argument finds its basis in the fact that the petroleum of Canada is wholly different from that of Pennsylvania. We know that the Canada oil rocks pass underneath Lake Erie, and lie (no doubt with their proper petroleum) at a great depth beneath the oil sands of the Allegheny river country. The results of the Geological Survey in 1875, will enable us to give, with great accuracy, the additional depth to which our wells would have to be sunk to broach Canada oil. Certainly the depth will be too great to affect our production. But the argument against any supposed connection of our oil with rocks at that depth will only be strengthened thereby.

The gas wells of the Erie shore are, doubtless, furnished by the Canadian oil horizon.

The scientific geological questions connected with the discussion of the 2,000 feet of measures exhibited in Mr. Lucas' profile section must be left for Mr. Carll's reports. Some of these require close work during the ensuing season. But enough is already known to make it safe to state here, that the "bluff sand rock" of the profile is, probably, the top of the Chemung formation No. VIII; that the Red Catskill formation No. IX, which forms arches in the gaps at Blairsville and Connellsville, and makes the great red terrace along the Allegheny mountain at Altoona and Tyrone, has thinned away to nothing;—that the White Catskill No. X, above it, is also almost gone;—that the lowest coal beds are in No. XI, the thin-edged representative of the great Red Shale formation which surrounds the anthracite coal basins*; and that the conglomerate of No. XII is here a very subordinate sand-rock, of no great thickness. The variations in this interesting formation, which we have always considered as the base of the productive coal measures, will be illustrated by the Map and Profile of Slippery Rock creek.

It only remains to state, that the Geological Survey is indebted to the courtesy of Col. J. D. Potts, president of the Empire Transportation Company, for the opportunity of publishing Mr. Lucas' valuable contribution to an accurate knowledge of our oil region. Col. Potts has promised to add the gift of an instrumental survey of all the pipe lines of the company when completed. No doubt the publication of these materials will incite other citizens of western Pennsylvania to contribute towards the annual report of 1875 equally valuable data. What is now wanted is not theories but facts: local facts; well authenticated facts; accurately measured facts. It is the business

*The subconglomerate Coal Measures of East Kentucky, and of Montgomery county, Virginia, belong here.

of the survey to study and collate these; and to extend local surveys until the whole field is understood. In the end, we will not only be possessed of a correct map of western Pennsylvania, but of a correct plan of its underground, everywhere. What is given in the report of 1874 will serve for a small sample of the kind of work to be done, the mode of doing it, and what may be expected to come of it.

Letter of Col. J. D. Potts.

1129 GIRARD STREET, PHILADELPHIA,
March 22, 1875.

To the State Geologist:

DEAR SIR:—Our company own an extensive system of Pipe Lines, reaching from the Butler branch of the West Pennsylvania railroad, in Butler county, to the neighborhood of Edenburg, in Clarion county. The cost of this system has been great, and early in 1874 it became desirable to form some idea as to the probable farther extension thereof becoming requisite through farther and new developments of oil territory.

It was also important to frame some probable conjecture as to the permanency of production in the territory which the existing system of our pipes traversed.

To accomplish these purposes I instructed Mr. Lucas, the Resident Engineer of our pipe system just described, to make a careful survey which should include a system of surface levels, having reference to mean tide as a datum, and which should also include the results found in drilling wells which were situated nearest to the line of survey. The latter information could, of course, only be obtained from the well owners, or those who had performed the drilling operations.

In many cases accurate records of the distances drilled through the various strata have not been kept, as such records were not essential to the main object which the well-owner had in view; but I believe, in the main, the information thus obtained can be relied upon.

The results of the whole survey were embraced in a condensed map of the district, and a longitudinal section.

The latter, you will notice, has been framed upon an assumed air line. This assumption, in cases where the line surveyed varied considerably from an air line, has led to a slight distortion, but not enough to seriously affect the object of the investigation.

I might say that we have not, since the survey, made any considerable extension of our pipe system; and further, that the southern extremity of the survey did not commence at the Butler branch, but at a point called the O'Connor well, some 3½ miles north-east thereof; this well being the most south-westerly one then producing in the district.

Very respectfully yours,

JOS. D. POTTS, *President.*

III.

On a Map and Profile of Coal and Oil Measures along Slippery Rock Creek, in Lawrence County, Pennsylvania; from a survey, in 1864, *by J. P. Lesley and Leo Lesquereux.*

Ten years ago the writer was called upon to explain the cause of the failure of oil operations along the lower reach of Slippery Rock creek, where several wells had been sunk to depths exceeding 700 and 800 feet.

It became evident that the only *assignable* reason for failure was that the wells were not deep enough, and should be sunk to 1,500 feet, more or less, to strike the third sand of the Venango county petroleum measures. This conclusion was confirmed by the facts revealed by the oil sinkings of 1873, in Butler county, as displayed in the profile section of Mr. Lucas; Article II of this volume.

The map and profile of Slippery Rock is now published because it explains certain points in the geology of Western Pennsylvania, not commonly known; viz:

1. The relation of the mountain sand rock series to the productive coal measures above them is well exhibited.

2. The local thinning away to nothing of No. XII, a massive and sometimes conglomeritic sand formation, as large (normally) as the heaviest of the oil sands, affords a visible illustration which may be studied in the open air, and as flagrant an example as will be likely to occur anywhere underground, of those irregularities in thickness and coarseness which characterize all the sand rocks, both those of the oil series and of the mountain series, and by which the history of petroleum production has been entirely determined.

3. The issue of petroleum from the base of No. XII, on Slippery Rock creek, as in Eastern Kentucky,* repeats the argument for the genesis of petroleum in its home rock, at whatever horizon in the series that may lie in any given region.

*See my paper in Proceedings Amer. Philos. Soc. Philada., Vol. X., p. 39, extracted below.

4. The same steady and consistent, but slightly irregular, dip of all the measures to the southward, seen in this section as in the profile of Mr. Lucas, finds here another opportunity for its measurement. The top of the principal (bluff?) sand in well No. 17, at Seceder's Bridge, lies 160 feet *above* the datum level of the profile, water level at the junction of Slippery Rock and of Conequeness. The top of the same sand in well No. 1, at Van Gordon's bridge, lies 100 feet *below* the same datum level.

Distance, 26,000′. Fall, 260′. Rate, 1′: 100′.
Mean rate per mile, 53′; S. 35° W.

The shape of the water-tree of the Slippery Rock and Conequenessing basin shows that this (S. 35° W.) is the bearing of maximum dip of the underground, considering only the mountain sand rocks next below the present surface.

Slippery Rock creek, in descending from Seceder's bridge to Van Gordon's bridge, follows a somewhat tortuous course, which lengthens the air-line of 26,000 to 30,000 feet. The water-fall amounts to 130 feet, which gives a rate of 23′ per mile. Taken on the 26,000′ air-line, the creek descends at a rate of 26′ per mile. The mean dip of the sand-rock is therefore just twice that of the water-fall.

Hence, at Seceder's bridge the *bottom* of the conglomerate sand-rock (No. XII) ranges along at a height of fifty feet above the bed of the creek;—in three-quarters of a mile it descends to the bed of the creek;—for a mile and a quarter further down it is covered by the creek;—for another mile it keeps just at the level of the creek;—and for yet another mile it keeps a little above the creek. For four miles the Slippery Rock flows in a small canyon, with vertical walls, composed of the outcrop of No. XII; and there is thus afforded a fine opportunity of studying the variations and irregularities of one of these great sand-rock formations not to be neglected by oil men.

The rock in question, then, No. XII, is at Seceder's bridge 104 feet thick;—three-quarters of a mile below the bridge, where its bottom touches water level, 80 feet;—and three miles below the bridge, only 30 feet. Whether it thins away to nothing, or whether it gets unnoticed below water-level and eludes further study, will be seen hereafter.

5. The next important thing to notice is the appearance of gravel layers in the body of No. XII at Seceder's bridge. Two of these gravel layers are represented in the profile section: one, at the base of the sand-rock, XII; the other towards the top of it. They do not exactly underlie each other; the thin edge of the upper one lapping over the thin edge of the lower one.

This illustrates what happens in the oil sands of the oil regions to the north-east. It is in such lenticular patches and streaks of gravel, or conglomerate, in the body of the oil sand rocks, that the great accumulations of petroleum are struck by the flowing and spouting wells. Wherever wells are sunk outside of the thinned edges of these gravel patches they find the sand-rock too compact, and such wells are sure to be either poor or dry, whether the sand-rock be charged with oil or not.

The Slippery Rock, which gave name to this fine stream at the first settlement of the country, is a plate of sandstone lying in place on the east bank, about a mile above Van Gordon's bridge, where there was a natural exudation of petroleum.

An old natural oil spring is marked on the map at *l*, three miles above Van Gordon's bridge, just below the mouth of Hell Hollow. An old well, 20 feet deep, was here sunk, but the petroleum issues from the base of No. XII, and does not rise through any fissure from the oil sand rocks which underlie the bed of the creek at a depth of 1,000 feet or more.

6. From Gordon's bridge, down stream, there is a remarkable change in the structure. This change has caused the stream to turn out of its natural course towards the west, and, after joining the Conequenessing, to flow north of west.

Where two streams of size meet full in each other's face, flowing in nearly horizontal strata, the geologist may be sure that he will find the bottom of a wide and gentle trough. Both streams flow down the dip. The dip on the Conequenessing above its junction with the Slippery Rock must be the reverse of that on the Slippery Rock. In other words, the long gentle descent S. 35° W. of the rocks which we have been describing along the Slippery Rock, and which is exhibited in the section, ceases between Van Gordon's bridge and Wirtemburg, and gives place to horizontality, or to a gentle rise, which continues up the Conequenessing.

To show this, nine little vertical sections have been placed on the map along the banks of the two streams. They show a sandstone layer, the *bottom* of which is 10 feet above water, 2,400′ below the bridge; 30 feet, 1,400′ further; 60 feet, 600′ further; 50 feet, 1,350′ further; 70 feet, 1,300′ further; 66 feet, 2,200′ further; and 60 feet, 1,900′ still further down, where Smaley's run enters the Conequenessing. Taking the fall of water into consideration, and the variable thickness of the sandstone layer in question, and confining our attention to the right bank alone, we may say that the dip in the hill side above water level, *rises* at Wirtemburg about 40′ in a distance of half a mile, in a direction about S. 75° W., and then slowly *falls* westward down the Conequenessing.

But the variability of the sandstone stratum which gives us this dip is sometimes extraordinary. At Wirtemburg the bottom of the rock is 30 feet above the water on both sides of the stream, but the layer is only 6′ thick on the right bank, and much thicker on the left. Further down it is thicker on the right bank. At the mouth of the stream the bottom of the rock is 50′ above water, right, and only 10′ left; but the stratum is only 4′ thick, right, and 30′ thick, left. The sand-rock, therefore, at this point, swells from 4 to 30 feet in thickness in about 200 yards. As no material general disturbance of dip is here supposable, these figures show that it is the *bottom* of the sand-rock which swells downwards 40 feet, while the *top* sinks only 14 feet.

Mr. Wrigley expresses his belief that *all* variations of thickness in the oil sands, or rather in the oil gravels, are variations of the bottom plane, and not of the top plane, of the rock. In one sense this is theoretically true, because the extra force of a current depositing gravel should be first exerted in excavating the sand and mud upon which it throws down its gravel. But until a very large number of observed cases be collected it would be unsafe to lay it down as a rule to govern practical cil operations, that the bottom plane of an oil rock is the plane of irregularity. If, however, such a rule be proven, then it will follow that in calculations of dip the well records of the *bottom* of a rock must not be taken into account, but only the well records of the *top*. In the case of the rock under consideration it will appear, by what is reported of it below, that neither its top surface nor its bottom surface can be assumed as a regular plane, from which to get the *grand mean* of dip of the underground country of the region.

Mr. Carll's underground contour lines of the first and third oil sands of Venango will illustrate the above remarks, but must be carried out to a greater extent than was possible in 1874 before the question can be fully settled.

The Wirtemburg sandstone thickens to 12′ half a mile above Smalley's run, and to 23′ at the mouth of Smalley's run, where the upper 17′ of it is gravel and the lower 6′ sand. Near the mouth of Conequenessing, on the Beaver river, it is from 60 to 75 feet thick, and well developed into two gravel-sand formations, with a streak of coal between. It has always been recognized here as the genuine conglomerate No. XII.

In all this distance, from Seceder's bridge, down the Slippery Rock and down the Conequenessing, to Beaver river, we are never at a loss in our structure, because the ferriferous (iron ore bearing) limestone crops out on the hill-sides above. We have seen that at Seceder's bridge this limestone is 6′ thick and 215′ above the water; at Van Gordon's bridge, 3¼′ and 155′ above the water; and on Beaver river, 19′ and 227′ above the water.

Distance 26,000′. Fall 190′. Rate 1′: 137′.
Mean dip of limestone per mile 38½′ S. 35° W.

The bottom of XII is below the limestone at Seceder's bridge 165′; on Beaver river about 200′; therefore, at Wirtemburg, where the limestone is 155′ above the water, XII must either be just under water; or it must be the little sand-rock above described, 10′ above the water, which no doubt it is.

Mr. Lesquereux, at my request, made his own independent observations on the continuity of No. XII, but with an entirely different object in view, an object to be mentioned directly. He identified the Beaver-river-outcrop of No. XII, gradually thinning as it was followed up the Conequenessing, with the great Seceder-bridge-outcrop, gradually thinning as it was followed down the Slippery Rock; and he came to the conclusion that this important, massive, often conglomeratic and almost universally outspread formation—well worthy to be regarded as the base of the productive coal measures—actually thins away and entirely disappears for a distance of five miles along Slippery Rock above Wirtemburg.

As this phenomenon is typical of what must take place in other parts of the State, and explains the source of many former geological errors, and as such irregularities and vacancies must also be characteristic of the mountain sands and the oil sands which underlie this sand of No. XII, the following summary of Mr. Lesquereux's careful observations is here added.* He says:

At Homewood station No. XII is exposed along the river, with a thickness of 160′, resting on No. XI soft black shales, with a layer of ball ore (clay-iron-stone) and thin layers of coal. At Homewood furnace and the mouth of Conequenessing, XII is 110′ thick, on XI shales and ore. At the mouth of Smalley, six miles up Conequenessing, XII over XI, are together 60′ thick. At the mouth of Slippery Rock XII is 40′ thick, only 6′ or 8′ of XI being visible above water. Ascending Slippery Rock, rapid irregularities are noticable, the massive XII turning into one or two layers of shaley sandstone, disappearing and appearing again. It is last seen just below the lower mill at Wirtemburg, as a six foot stratum of grit, overlying 6′ or 8′ of black shales and ore. Here "it definitely loses itself in a thin bed of soft shaly sandstone, wedging into the top of that clay iron ore which in the section is marked as under the bed of coal." These strata (XI) continue along the creek, above Wirtemburg, at the same horizon and with the same character, but without any trace of sandstone (XII) *for six miles above.* Then XII re-appears in the same manner and at the same geological horizon (*i. e.* lying upon XI) as it was seen to disappear at Wirtemburg. It rapidly increases in thickness, and at Seceder's bridge (three miles further up) XII is already 110′ thick, lying on 49′ of XI.

Mr. Lesquereux made one of his most important fossil discoveries in tracing this outcrop. To explain this the following section of the Wirtemburg hillside, as he gives it, must be carefully studied.

The Wirtemburger Section.

Capping the hills are fragmentary patches of a once extensive coal measure rock, (Freeport S. S.,) a hard, gritty, micacious sand-

* See his memoir "On Fucoides in the Coal Formations," with a plate, read before the American Philosophical Society, Philadelphia, May 18, 1866, and published at p. 313, of Vol. XIII, of the Transactions.

stone, generally gravelly in its upper layers.* Its lower layer, somewhat shaly, is marked by abundant fucoid (seaweed) *prints*, for no trace of the plant itself has been left. The prints are moulds left by the decay of marine Algæ, resembling Hall's *large Palæophycus tubularis*† whose place has been filled by a softer whitish sand. Accordingly the original form of the plants are pretty distinctly printed on the stone. The moulds are generally placed horizontally on the stones, but sometimes penetrate obliquely or even vertically. Omitting for the present a description of these fucoids, the next formation, *descending* the hillsides, consists of shales in great force, including streaks of coal, and thin beds of stigmaria fire-clay and shaly sandstone. The whole mass is about 175′ thick, of which 150′ are shales; soft, slightly micaceous and spotted black by oxide of iron, containing in places a quantity of branching, cylindrical fucoids, mostly resembling Hall's *small palæophycus tubularis.*‡

In some places the seams of coal become workable beds, 3 and 4 feet thick, as shown in the profile section.

Limestone 3 feet thick, hard and black, underlies the shales. It shows no remains of plants. It rests, like a coal bed, on

Fire-clay, 2 feet thick. This rests on

Sandstone, 5 feet thick, sometimes passing into a hard mixture of coarse fire-clay and leaves and stems of stigmaria. In fact the whole seven feet of rock beneath the limestone may be considered as a thick bed of fire-clay, the top part nicer than the rest. Under it come

Shales, 15 feet thick, soft, grayish, without a trace of fossil plants. Under this lies another and remarkable

Limestone, 1 foot thick at Wirtemburg, and then

Coal, 5″ to 1′ thick, bituminous, hard, laminated, sometimes bony or shaly. Then

Black shale, 5 to 8 feet thick, soft, easily disintegrated, intermixed with small oval pebbles or balls of carbonate iron ore, and the top of the shale sometimes becoming a layer of clay iron stone balls. This is at low water level at Wirtemburg.

The lower limestone, coal and black shale continue in view for five miles above Wirtemburg, along the creek, wherever erosion

*See profile section between wells No. 2 and No. 3.

†Hall's Palæon. New York, I. p. 7, pl. 2, figs. 1 and 2.

‡Palæon., New York, I. p. 7, pl. 2, figs. 1, 2, 4, 5.

exposes the rocks; and the limestone never exceeds 18″, and always exhibits a certain kind of fossil plant, now to be described, named by Mr. Lesquereux, on this discovery at Wirtemburg, in 1865, *caulerpites marginatus.*

The bottom of the limestone is the base of the carboniferous system proper. The top of the black shale is the top of the subcarboniferous system proper.

Between the limestone, with its *caulerpites marginatus*, and the black shale, with its pebbles of iron ore and thin coal, *ought to* come in the "great conglomerate" No. XII. But it is here wholly absent--evidently was never deposited; although it is over 100 feet thick only three miles up the creek and 150 feet thick ten miles down the stream.

Water plants of the family of the Algæ or fucoids, or sea-weeds, are remarkably scarce in the coal measures. In 1836, Thompson could mention only *one species*, at the end of a catalogue of 39 genera and 290 species fossil plants of the coal measures. From 1836 to 1865, no fossil botanist had added a single carboniferous fucoid to the list. Some doubtful forms were published by Mr. Lesquereux, in Silliman's Journal, Vol. 32, p. 194, and Professor Stevenson and Mr. White have recently found *spirophyton* or *cock's tail* forms high up in the coal measures.

In 1865, however, Mr. Lesquereux found large numbers of them on the underside of the Wirtemburg lower limestone. He says:

"They were found attached or flattened on the lower surface of a thin stratum of limestone immediately overlaying a bed of coal 6′ to 18′ thick. The fucoides, for they belong evidently to a kind of marine plants, have thus grown, either as a part of the materials of which the coal is a compound, or immediately over them. For they appear to derive the black color, which seemingly paints them on the limestone, rather from the coal than from their own substance. When detached blocks of the limestone have fallen into the creek, and, washed for a time, have been cleared of the coal which adheres to the lower surface, the matter becomes bleached, and the remains of the fucoides appear in slightly depressed and dark distinct outlines. But when the coal which adheres to the limestone, as if it were strongly glued to it, is removed by mechanical force, the stone preserves its black color, and the remains of these plants are scarcely discernible.

"The limestone on the line of contact with the coal, and for two or three inches above it, is somewhat shaly, though of a piece and homogeneous, its thickness varying from 12 to 18 inches. It is a kind of "black-band" (iron ore) containing iron and sulphur in large proportions, and essentially composed of *broken remains of innumerable marine shells.* The fucoides, which occupy only a few inches of the lower and shaly part of this limestone, *are mixed with the remains of shells, and often perforated and lacerated by them.*

"Though hard, compact and in banks generally continuous, the limestone layer breaks into large cuboidal pieces.

"*Caulerpites marginatus* (new species) is the name of these fucoidal remains. Their form, however variable, may be compared to that of a lyre or harp. * * * * The fronds vary in length from two inches to one foot, are half as long as broad, and surrounded by an apparently fleshy or tubular margin from ⅛ to ¼ inch broad. Strongly arched ribs, apparently produced by alternate inflation and thinning of substance, pass from the inner side of the vein to the other border, filling the whole lamina. * * * * They are **not** true nerves, for they do not branch or connect with each other. They abruptly vary, * * * * an appearance likely caused by the compression of a body somewhat inflated like a bladder."

Mr. Lesquereux remarks, after a full description (with plates) on the resemblance of these plants to the well known and far older *Fucoides Cauda-galli,* (Cock's tail sea-weed,) discovered by Vanuxem in 1835, in the lowest Devonian formation of New York, (splendid specimens of which may be seen on the limestone rocks at Tyrone City,) called afterward by Mr. James Hall *Spirophyton,* (Corkscrew plant.)

Mr. Lesquereux, after discussing Mr. Hall's ideas of the structure of the plant, remarks its *apparent* resemblance to *Thalassiophyllum clathrus,* (lattice Sea-leaf,) growing on the shores of Russian America; but considers it quite a different sort of plant, not at all bushy, and altogether more simple. He therefore finds a place for it in the living group of green-seed sea-weeds, called *Caulerpæ;* which he describes as having a horny, membranous substance, destitute of calcareous matter, without cells, and strengthened inside with a spongy network of filaments, filled with a sort of slime. The stalks printed on the Wirtemburg limestone are shining and polished, and the whole plant was fossilized as a flattened flexible bag.

Brogniart describes a *Fucoides serra,* from the extremely old limestone rocks of Point Levy, (Quebec,) which must have had a similar growth, but a different shape.

These *Caulerpites marginatus* of the lower Wirtemburg limestone differ entirely from Hall's *Palæophycus* (ancient sea-weed) *tubularis,* both the small variety, so plentiful in the shales high up the Wirtemburg hill side, and the large variety in the sandstone at the very top of the hills, described a few pages back. The latter (large variety) are somewhat thicker than those of the shales (small variety,) varying in thickness from one-half to one inch; either simple, like flexuous pipes; or irregularly forking on one side only; or divided from a central axis, and sending branches in every direction.

It is observable that although the shales of this Wirtemburg section are mostly soft, grayish, apparently well fitted for the preservation of coal plants, there is not, in the whole 165 feet, any trace of ferns, or of any of the species of land plants generally and commonly found in the coal measures. At one place only, just below the mill one mile below Wirtemburg, a shaly sandstone, seen parting the two benches of the coal bed at the base of the section, bears prints of the bark of Calamites, (reed,) Lepidodendron, (scale-tree,) and Sigillaria, (seal-marked tree.) The *Caulerpites* limestone forms the roof of this coal bed.

So the *Archimedes* fossil-bearing limestones (upper bed and sometimes next lower bed) rest on shaly sands, marked with large coal plants and holding thin layers of coal, in Kentucky, Illinois and Arkansas. These *Archimedes* limestones are *sub*-carboniferous formations, corresponding to our No. XI and No. X.

The fossil *palæophycus tubularis* covering the soft shales of the Wirtemburg hill-sides and printed on the upper conglomerate sandstone on the hill-tops, are also like those to be seen in Chemung (?) rocks (No. VIII,) along Oil Creek, in Venango county, Pa., and in Waverly sandstone. No. X, in Ohio, and seem to be identical species.

Judging by all this, Mr. Lesquereux's first impression naturally was that all the rocks of our profile section from the bed of the creek to the tops of the hills belonged to the subcarboniferous system, and the conglomerate sand-rock capping the hills looked like No. XII, the base of the productive coal measures or carboniferous system proper. This conclusion being utterly inadmissible, and shown to be so in the locality itself by his personal tracing of the real No. XII, as above described, from Homewood station to Wirtemburg and Seceder's bridge, there resulted the following important conclusions:

1. The Slippery Rock section exhibits 300 feet of the lower productive coal measures, in a large degree destitute of carboniferous land plants; but, on the other hand, largely charged with sea-plants belonging to an older (subcarboniferous) age.

2. The sea plants of this kind began to live as early as the lower Silurian age, (Calciferous No. II,) and represent the primordial types of the vegetable world. They continued to flourish through the upper Silurian age, (Clinton, No. V,) as *Fucoides antiquus*, (*Buthopteris antiquata*, *gracilis*, *palmata*, *impudica* and *ramosa* of Hall.) They were especially abundant in the Devonian age, (Chemung and Waverly, No. VIII and X.) They continued to grow as *palæophycus tubulosus* in the lower true coal measure age, (Allegheny R. Coal System.) And they reappear as *Fucoides Targioni* (Brogt) in the Chalk age of Europe.

The other type of fossil sea plants discovered by Mr. Lesquereux, at the base of our section, viz: *Caulerpites marginatus*, is represented throughout the whole extent of the Devonian rocks. At least it seems identical with the *fucoides cauda-galli*, of the Corniferous, (Upper Helderburg, bottom of VIII,) and similar forms in the Chemung (top of VIII) and in the Waverly (X.) It is especially abundant in S. E. Kentucky, about 50 feet below the base of the millstone grit (Conglomerate No. XII.) There may have been different species, but certainly most of the marine Algæ had a large vertical time-range through the Palæozoic formations.

3. Consequently they cannot be used as geological guides. We know nothing about their internal structure. They were cellular masses, easily rotted, rapidly losing shape when dead, and leaving

on the ancient shore-sand mere moulds or indistinct impressions. They cover, by millions, the Chemung rocks (Oil system,) and have a thousand shapes which seem, at first, to be easily classified into species and genera; but the task is fruitless; form graduates into form, and no specific marks can be detected. Whole fields of this ancient marine vegetation appear like a grass-plot, each blade of which has some peculiar feature, but none marked enough to make it positively distinct. Either there are as many species as individuals, or all belong to one species, represented by a great number of closely allied varieties. They cannot be used as geological guides.

It is entirely different with the land plants of the coal ages, whose woody tissue was well fossilized, the leaves retaining their specific outline and nerve structure, and trunks, branches, leaves and fruit all offering themselves for study to the botanist. Hence Mr. Lesquereux's life-long labor to classify the coal plants in relation to the coal beds, so that the geologist might find in the special vegetation of each bed a key to its identification all over a coal basin.

Sea-plants have always lived in an element less subject to variations of heat and cold than land plants exposed to shifting north and south, sea and land winds. Hence sea-weed forms have remained more constant from the earliest ages; whereas the air breathing coal plants were subject to violent extremes from age to age, as the continent was alternately submerged to receive sand-gravel deposits, and exposed again to sustain a forest. Changes of species and genus must have followed the covering up of every principal coal bed.

Sometimes the new land was sand, and sometimes mud; therefore, sometimes the soil was warm and sometimes cold; sometimes calcereous and fertile, sometimes barren. All such changes would change the vegetation; and hence the different qualities of coal beds.

Migrations of plants must have occurred, as various localities were submerged and others were laid dry. No one species needs have perished entirely; but the groupings of the species must have varied frequently, and hence one coal bed in a region should be characterized by a certain botanical *aspect*, produced by the predominance of one or more species of plants over the rest at that time and over that area.

4. As coal beds are now acknowledged by all men of science to be fossilized fields of ancient air-breathing vegetation, consisting of trees, reeds, ferns and mosses; and as there seems much good reason to believe that cannel coal beds (from which petroleum can be distilled) differ from them chiefly in this, that the vegetable mass was not fibrous, but cellular; that is, were not air-breathing, but water plants; so there is a strong disposition among geologists to explain the origin of fluid petroleum, held by oil sands and oil shales, by a reference to the proofs we have of an extraordinary submarine vegetation in the Devonian age.

"There is no doubt," says Mr. Lesquereux, "that the marine vegetation of the Palæozoic ages can be compared for luxuriance, and in some measure for its composition also, to the terrestrial vegetation of the coal epoch. From the upper Devonian down to the lower Silurian, some strata of shales are not only covered, but indeed filled, sometimes for hundreds of feet in thickness, with fossilized forms of water-plants (Hydrophytes.) These evidences of a primordial vegetable world are far more numerous than the remains of land plants in the shales of the coal measures. Nevertheless, they appear to belong to plants of a soft tissue, mere cellular, probably mostly uncellular vegetables, the debris of which had not by much the same chances of fossilization.*

*Mr. Lesquereux ascribes this luxuriance to the "acknowledged" surplus of carbonic acid in the air and water of the early geological ages. I, for one, am not willing to acknowledge this assumption. Peat bogs are now as deep and probably as quick growing as any of the coal beds. Why are not the thickest coal measures those of the oldest age? Why was there an immensely long non coal bed producing age between the Juniata (Hamilton) coal measures, and the Appalachian (carboniferous) coal measures? Why are there no Silurian coal measures? Is not the marine vegetation now as luxuriant as that of any previous age? Do not the hydrozoa require as much carbon as the hydrophyta? and are they not as abundant now as ever? If an excess of carbonic acid occurred in the coal era, where did the excess come from? If from the nebulous envelope of the earth, why did its effects not show earlier? If from volcanic exhalations, why do we find that the coal era was one of remarkable freedom from structural disturbance of the earth crust? These and such like questions make the whole carbonic acid gas theory extremely questionable. *Quantity* of coal can be just as easily explained by reference to immensely long ages of unusual quietness and steadiness of the relative level of land and sea, with the ordinary amount of moisture and heat in the atmosphere. Time to collect and fix a moderate quantity of carbonic acid is as good as having an extra quantity of carbonic acid.

"We have no proofs from fossil remains that the Hydrophytes (water plants) of old attained a very large size. The largest circular fronds of *Fucoides cauda-galli* show a diameter of about one foot; the greatest depth of the branching Fucoides in the Chemung is from two to three feet. But we cannot judge all the vegetable representatives of an epoch from a few fossilized specimens. These may have belonged to a species of a more compact organization, or to some kind of Coralines, which had their surface covered with a hard crust of lime, while other groups of a soft, mere cellular tissue, which had representatives of a large size, have been totally decomposed and destroyed. There is no need, however, of this hypothesis, on the size of the Palæozoic Algæ, to argue by comparison on the fecundity of the marine vegetation of old. Small species of Hydrophytes in our time afford sufficient analogies. The great bank of *Sargassum*, which extends between the 20th and 45th parallel of latitude, covers, according to Humboldt's computation, a space of more than 260,000 square miles. In places this floating bank is so thick as to arrest the progress of vessels, and it appears at present to be of the same extent and to occupy the same place as when it was first noticed by navigators. What can we then infer to have been the result of a vegetation whose force was at least double of what it is now, and which has written its history in whole strata of great thickness?

"It cannot be presumed that this whole vegetable world of Palæozoic seas has left nothing after it but useless petrified remains." The inference is natural that as the land plants produced our coal beds, the sea plants produced our petroleum. The function of both was the same, to fix and store up the carbon of the air for futurity, and their different constitution enabled them to do it, one in the air, the other in the sea.

Chemistry teaches little about this subject in a direct way.* But we may get an indication from the natural chemistry of life. "Algæ, especially the group of the *Caulerpæ*, feed some of the animals of the seas remarkable for the size and the prodigious fatness of their bodies. Harvey suggests that the green fat of

*Liebig wrote to Lesquereux that there were, unhappily, no analyses of species of Fucus, or of other Hydrophytes, which could be used as affording support to his views, but that his arguments were so conclusive that they had removed any doubt in his (Liebig's) mind of the truth of the theory.

the turtle, so highly prized by epicures, may be colored by the unctuous green juice of the Caulerpæ on which they feed. It is quite possible that the color of the Devonian petroleum, which is exactly that of the Chlorosperm Hydrophytes, may be explained in the same manner. Whales are not certainly known to feed on Algæ, but their stomachs are always found filled with them."

This leads to another consideration. There is a remarkable analogy between the gelatinous sea animals and the gelatinous water plants. Whales are known to be habitual feeders on squids, or cuttle fish, some of which are small and others of immense size, and on all the families of the great world of jelly fish. Many who doubt that petroleum is the decomposed and recomposed hydro-carbon organism of the seaweed world, are strongly inclined to assert that it is the decomposed and recomposed hydro-carbon organism of the world of coral and jelly fish life. Geologists have noticed that the casts of corals in the New York and Upper Canada rocks, underlying our Pennsylvania oil formations, are often filled with the Canadian kind of petroleum. The corniferous limestone, full of fossil animal forms, is roundly asserted by many to be the home of the Canada oil; and some go so far as to assign to it the source of the Pennsylvania oils, by an ascending distillation. The arguments against this view have already been given. But it shows how deeply rooted in the minds of all who know most about the whole subject, is the conviction that petroleum is nothing but the fossil product of the soft sea animals and sea vegetables; no doubt of both. But the older and deeper (Canadian and Middle Kentucky) oils are more animal, and the upper (Pennsylvania) oils are more vegetable.

To give this statement all the breadth it deserves would require a small volume. Mr. Lesquereux has resumed it in a few admirably written paragraphs at the close of his memoir, which leave little to be said. He heads the statement thus:

Geological and Geographical Distribution of Petroleum Deposits and Fucoidal Remains.

"Oil bearing strata are seen in the coal measures mostly inferior to the big bed of coal, No. 1, which is often a cannel coal;

and sometimes also, but rarely, at a higher horizon, as, for example, below coal No. 3, and also No. 12*, generally in more or less evident connection with cannel coal. This has probably led to the opinion, still admitted by some geologists, that all the deposits of petroleum owe their origin to a slow decomposition of coal under some peculiar influences. As there has not heretofore been observed any indications that remains of marine plants might have existed at some places, mixed with aerial plants of the bogs of the coal epoch, it was not easy to account for such a phenomenon as that of the formation of coal and petroleum at the same horizon and under the same circumstances. But this curious fact, I think, is explicable now. When the combustible matter has been formed especially from the remains of aerial plants, whose tissue was mostly vascular, or vascular and cellular, like that of the *Lepidodendron*, *Sigillaria*, ferns, etc., it becomes by mineralization a hard coal, with thin layers or distinct laminas, sometimes shining, sometimes mixed with opaque layers and flakes of charcoal, and giving, by combustion, a proportion of ashes according to the nature of the wood. When it has been formed merely by floating fresh-water vegetables, like *Stigmaria* and its leaves, the compound, originally half fluid and more easily decomposed, becomes, by the slow process of combustion, compact, homogeneous, without apparent layers, tending to mere bitumen, thus forming the different varieties of cannel coal. Now, I believe that when this floating vegetation has been more or less densely intermixed with marine plants, and perhaps also influenced by marine water, the almost total absence of woody fibres has casually prevented the bedding of the material, and so, by slow maceration, part of it has been transformed into fluid bitumen. It is probably for this reason that we sometimes see, as at Breckenridge, in Kentucky, a bed of cannel coal so nearly decomposed into petroleum that it can scarcely be used as coal, and at a lower level, even in close proximity, and where every trace of coal has disappeared, inferior strata of sandstone, strongly impregnated with petroleum.

*These are the numbers adopted by the Kentucky Geologists. The Pennsylvania coal beds were lettered, not numbered. But in both cases coal bed A, and coal bed No. 1, means the lowest bed of the Productive Coal Measures.

"In descending from the base of the coal measures into the Devonian, we find deposits of oil nearly in the whole thickness of this formation, with the exception of the Old Red sandstone, equivalent of the Ponent* and part of the Vespertine of Pennsylvania. All the plants of this formation, and they are numerous enough, belong to swamp or land plants, and no trace of petroleum has been seen in these measures. But down from this red sandstone, the Chemung is full of remains of Fucoides, and where they are found, all the sandstone strata of this formation are more or less impregnated with oil.

"Still lower the black shales of the Hamilton group are so much charged with bitumen, that they have often been considered as the true source of the Devonian petroleum. There the remains are nearly, almost totally, obliterated. A few teeth of fishes and small shells, very rarely large trunks of *Lepidodendron*, nothing more, at least in those extensive deposits, generally of great thickness, which border our western coal basins. The color of these shales, and the bitumen which they contain, indicate a formation under water, under the influence of a powerful vegetation; and a marine vegetation, without doubt; else, besides the well-preserved trunks of *Lepidodendron*, which have probably been brought floating, we should find there other remains of aerial plants. At Worthington, in Ohio, where I have spent much time in searching for fossil remains in these black shales, I have seen them often covered with round spots of coaly matter, varying in diameter from half an inch to one foot, showing no trace of organism, and resembling some kind of round, hard Ulvaceæ, like those which are seen in great quantity attached to the muddy shores in shallow water.†

*Ponent. H. D. Rogers' name for No. IX, which is several thousand feet thick in Eastern Pennsylvania, but thinsto nothing under Western Pennsylvania. Vespertine is No. X, also one or two thousand feet thick at the East, but represented only by some thin layers of sand and shale in the West. These two formations make the Second Mountain at Mauch Chunk and Pottsville; the upper half of the Back Bone Allegheny Mountain; most of the Catskill Mountain on the Hudson; &c. The Chemung, Portage and Hamilton, No. VIII, make the Valley of Williamsport, Lock Haven, Altoona, &c., along which at numerous points slight traces of petroleum have been noticed.

†Only in one region have true coal measures and coal beds been found in the Hamilton, viz: on the lower Juniata River. Here an early air-breathing vegetation grew and flourished. The edge of one of these coal beds can be seen crossing the river at Millerstown about 30 miles above Harrisburg.

"Descending further down in the Lower Devonian and Upper Silurian, we see there also the rocks saturated with petroleum, and generally marked by an abundance of Fucoidal remains. It is probably from the rocks of the Upper Silurian that Prof. Brogniart obtained his Fucoides from Canada. In Ohio and other western States, where the Upper Silurian limestone is barren of remains, it does not show any deposits of petroleum. In Canada the same rocks have both Fucoides and fluid bitumen. Prof. Lesley, after an examination of the east end of Canada, Gaspe, wrote me (5th January, 1866): "All sorts of marine vegetation of Upper Silurian and Devonian ages seem there in great abundance, and petroleum everywhere in the Devonian, and oozing from the lower Helderburg limestone formation.

"Still deeper the Lower Silurian has small deposits of bitumen in cavities of limestone, even when every trace of organism has disappeared. This fact again is, I think, another indication of the relation of petroleum to a marine vegetation. For it is well understood that vegetable life has ruled the seas in its minute representatives, Diatomaceæ, Desmidiaceæ, long before animal life could be supplied or sustained by it. These diminutive and primitive oil reservoirs are attributable to the concentration and decomposition of a local surplus of that primordial vegetation.

"The geographical distribution of petroleum and that of the remains of marine Algæ present the same remarkable coincidence. At Oil creek, Slippery Rock creek, in the Chemung of Virginia, Ohio, Kentucky, everywhere indeed where oil has been seen, either in cavities or saturating the rocks, and where the strata were open to view, a remarkable amount of Fucoidal remains has been observed. This cannot be a mere casual coincidence.

"The discussion presented in the last part of this paper may then be closed by this assertion: That though the theory of the origin of petroleum from marine vegetables is not yet supported by direct experiments and conclusive proofs, the reasons in favor of it are weighty enough to merit due consideration. The more so, that if recognized true, the theory presents an important chapter of the history of petroleum, and may prove of great value in its application."

ALPHABETICAL INDEX.

INDEX TO ARTICLE II.

MAP AND SECTION OF PIPE LINE BY D. JONES LUCAS.

INDEX TO ARTICLE III.

REPORT OF SLIPPERY ROCK CREEK.

www.ingramcontent.com/pod-product-compliance
Lightning Source LLC
LaVergne TN
LVHW021418110826
845150LV00007B/1975

* 9 7 8 1 4 2 5 5 0 9 5 7 6 *